T0277190

Praise for *The Waggle Dance*

The Waggle Dance is a must-read for anyone looking to be supported through any season of life. For a mom of three, this book gave me confidence and inspiration to be the best parent I can be. Courtney's words spoke straight to my heart, and I look forward to sharing her stories with my own children one day.

—Mackenzie Hatala, Wife, Mom of Three,
Registered Nurse, Barre3 Mentor

In *The Waggle Dance*, Courtney is incredibly vulnerable throughout. She holds nothing back through her self-reflection within her stories and leans into various learnings and growth opportunities that she's collected throughout her life. Rather than praise her many strengths, this book highlights her self-identified imperfections with such honesty, which is completely admirable in sharing her journey. Recognizing that Courtney's aim is to offer her learnings to others, I feel grateful for the wisdom *The Waggle Dance* imparted to me.

—Jillian Chaklos, Married to High School Sweetheart,
Mom of Two Daughters, and Dog Mom

The Waggle Dance feels like a rich conversation over steaming mugs of coffee with your new best friend. Courtney's authentic voice and timeless wisdom will captivate your heart and help you find new meaning and comforting lessons in all of life's challenges, celebrations, and seasons. This beautiful book will stay with you long after you close its pages. You will leave deeply encouraged and newly inspired to share your *own* waggle dance with the world!

—Allison Trowbridge, Founder & CEO of
Copper Books, Author of *Twenty-Two*

The Waggle Dance will take you to a place where you can look at your own life and quickly understand the gift of experiences and lessons you have been uniquely given. Courtney's storytelling is relatable, actionable, and inspiring. And get that tissue box out—the letters she writes to her son at the end of each chapter will have you welling up!

—Fran Hauser, Bestselling Author, Speaker, Investor, Entrepreneur, and Mom of Two Boys

The Waggle Dance takes us on a delightful and often emotional journey through life's triumphs and tragedies, and it underscores the importance of relationships at every stage. We are introduced to an array of inspirational people, who provide unwavering support and meaningful life lessons throughout.

—Terry Rhadigan, Chairman of the Detroit Sports Commission, Husband, and Father

The Waggle Dance is a book that I could see myself going back to in many seasons of life. I love how the chapters outwardly list their purpose. The concept of "read this when . . ." made it feel like an inspiring life reference guide of sorts. Courtney's writing is refreshingly authentic and relatable; the way she connects scripture with letters to her son to wrap each chapter's message helps each lesson provoke deeper thought and personalize it with the reader. Reading this book gave me a healthy dose of inspiration, reminders of the many human experiences and emotions that connect us, and all the warm fuzzies. I loved it.

—Lindsay Irrer, Wife, Mom of Three and Detroit Barre3 Studio Owner

For anyone who has ever found themselves wondering, *Is it just me? Surely, I am not the only one, The Waggle Dance* is the perfect companion and buoy. As Courtney herself writes,

"There is power in authenticity," this book is full of the honest, transparent, vulnerable, and tender power that parents need to feel encouraged through their day-to-day lives. The book's namesake refers to forager bees sharing their knowledge through funky little dances, and it's the perfect analogy reminding us that the wonky, twisted, often unexpected moves our lives take have value and bring priceless insight to others when shared.

—Kelly Davis, Mother of Two and Owner
of Frecklefaced Adventures

The Waggle Dance is replete with reminders that the everyday is worth living, sharing, and bearing witness to. It helped me reconnect with meaningful moments of my past and view them from a new perspective. For a new mom, these are lessons that I will carry with me and share with my daughter as she grows.

—Catherine Martin, Mom, Wife, and Book Lover

Step into the world of Courtney's mesmerizing memoir, *The Waggle Dance*, where every page resonates with the essence of her remarkable journey. Courtney delicately weaves together raw emotion and captivating detail. Courtney invites readers to join her on an unforgettable expedition through life's twists and turns. As I devoured each word, I felt as though I was right there beside her, experiencing every moment, every triumph, and every challenge. Her ability to infuse her narrative with the hand of God's presence adds an extra layer of depth and meaning, reminding us of the divine guidance that shapes our paths. *The Waggle Dance* is not just a book—it's a soul-stirring odyssey that will leave you profoundly moved and endlessly inspired.

—Sheila Savageau, Wife, Mother, and Grandmother

THE
WAGGLE
DANCE

THE WAGGLE DANCE

HOW THE LANGUAGE OF BEES CAN
TRANSFORM YOUR LIFE'S EXPERIENCES
INTO YOUR GREATEST LESSONS

BY COURTNEY YOUNGS

Published by Copper Books, an imprint of Forefront Books, Nashville, Tennessee. Distributed by Simon & Schuster.

Scripture quotations marked CEV are from the Contemporary English Version®, copyright © 1995 American Bible Society. All rights reserved.

Scripture quotations marked ESV are from the ESV® Bible (The Holy Bible, English Standard Version®), copyright ©2001 by Crossway, a publishing ministry of Good News Publishers. Used by permission. All rights reserved.

Scripture quotations marked KJV are from the King James Version. Public domain.

Scripture quotations marked NABRE are taken from the New American Bible, revised edition © 2010, 1991, 1986, 1970 Confraternity of Christian Doctrine, Inc., Washington, DC. All Rights Reserved.

Scripture quotations marked NASB1995 are from the New American Standard Bible®, Copyright © 1960, 1971, 1977, 1995 by The Lockman Foundation. All rights reserved.

Scripture quotations marked NET are from the NET Bible® http://netbible.com, copyright ©1996, 2019 used with permission from Biblical Studies Press, L.L.C. All rights reserved.

Scripture quotations marked NIV are taken from the Holy Bible, New International Version®, NIV®, Copyright © 1973, 1978, 1984, 2011 by Biblica, Inc.™ Used by permission of Zondervan. All rights reserved worldwide.

Scripture quotations marked NIVUK are from the Holy Bible, New International Version® Anglicized, NIV® Copyright © 1979, 1984, 2011 by Biblica, Inc.® Used by permission. All rights reserved worldwide.

Scripture quotations marked NKJV are from the New King James Version®. ©1982 by Thomas Nelson. Used by permission. All rights reserved.

Scripture quotations marked NLT are from the Holy Bible, New Living Translation, copyright ©1996, 2004, 2015 by Tyndale House Foundation. Used by permission of Tyndale House Publishers, a Division of Tyndale House Ministries, Carol Stream, Illinois 60188. All rights reserved.

Library of Congress Control Number: 2024906660

Print ISBN: 978-1-63763-316-8
E-book ISBN: 978-1-63763-317-5

Cover Design by George Stevens, G Sharp Design LLC
Interior Design by PerfecType, Nashville, TN

Printed in the United States of America

All for my Little Bee.
This dream was made possible by a loving God, an incredible husband, and the best family and friends a woman could ask for. My love for you all has no end.

CONTENTS

CONTENTS

INTRODUCTION
Welcome to My Waggle Dance

There is a good chance that if you are reading this, you are learning about me for the first time. So, before you turn the page and learn about the depths of my soul and thoughts, as well as some incredibly personal details of my life, please allow me to introduce myself.

My name is Courtney. I am not a celebrity or a woman with thousands of followers on Instagram. I still do not fully understand the proper use of hashtags, what length jeans are in style, or how to perfect this week's latest TikTok makeup trend.

I am both a self-proclaimed and actively recovering perfectionist and planner who now, on most days, feels content when I have simply kept all the pieces together. Or at the very least, when I can remember where I put those pieces a few hours ago.

In so many ways, I am just like you.

At the time I am writing this, I am technically thirty-two years old, but my soul has always felt decades beyond that. In 2019 my grandmother passed away, shortly after I married my college boyfriend but just before I divorced him and found my forever person, Michael. Although expected, my grandmother's death still felt tragic. She was my closest friend, and her departure from this earth began one of the hardest seasons I have ever experienced.

In 2022 I married Michael, a man almost nineteen years older than me. That same year, and by the grace of God, I became a mother to a beautiful baby boy, who changed my life within moments of his arrival. In the last ten years, I have lived in four different states, had seven different jobs (all with the same company), and acquired some of the most beautiful friendships a woman could ever ask for.

Needless to say, the last decade has really packed a punch.

And at one point, it was a punch that brought me to my knees. I questioned who I was, what I wanted, and how in the world I would ever move forward.

It was a hard season, but I believe that hard seasons are our best teachers.

In this hard season, I found myself searching for meaning. Like most of us, I had a desperate desire to see how the dots connected. I wanted to know what the plan was, what my purpose was, and how to combine the two to live the fullest life possible. Some would have called that ambitious; others would have labeled it senseless. I guess I believed it was somewhere right in the middle.

I think the good news is that, as part of my introspective journey, I learned to focus less on my own plans and more on God's, broke up with several old versions of myself, and am finally starting to feel like my own person. Most days.

But it was not without the help of a lot of people in my life. Both past and present.

For years I kept a list in my head—and eventually on my phone—that consisted of my favorite quotes, Bible verses, experiences, or words of advice that had been shared with me by people I loved and respected. Over time, that list grew and eventually became the foundation on which I started to rebuild. It was a simple list that with one glance reminded me of all the goodness in my life. And it became the guiding theory for this book.

One day I was talking on the phone to one of my best friends, Kyle. She and I had been friends for years and often spent many long hours in conversation grappling with the meaning of life and wondering aloud how to fulfill our unique purposes. I shared the list I had created, and I told her the purpose it had served in my life and how I had a gnawing feeling that somehow, I needed to pay this goodness forward.

At the time, Kyle was also knocking on the door of her next big adventure. She was preparing to leave her comfortable corporate job to pursue her dream of becoming a lawyer. Which made perfect sense, because not only is she one of the most intellectual people I have ever met, but she has a vocabulary that often requires me to do an internet search to understand her. Plus she has a wit that can barely be matched.

Above all, Kyle has always had an ability to take my ideas and make them better. It is something I used to resent but now truly love most about her. In fact, I am now a proud recipient of all her better ideas she shares with me.

Especially this one.

You see, when I explained my growing list and its value in my life, without pause Kyle told me it sounded a lot like a waggle dance.

Baffled and intrigued by her words, I later found myself searching the internet to learn more about what this kind of dance was. I thought to myself, *If Kyle really knew me, she would know that I had two left feet and only dance when socially lubricated.* Thankfully, after a brief moment spent educating myself about the life of bees, I realized that she was onto something, and the best part was that it required absolutely no rhythm on my part.

Waggle dance is a term used in beekeeping to describe the dance that forager bees use to share information with other bees about where to go for resources like food, water, or a nest. After the bee learns the information, they come back, do a fun little figure-eight dance for their friends, and share with them what they know so that they, too, can survive.

And that is both the start and end of what I know about bees or beekeeping. But it feels like enough. Thanks to my much wiser—and definitely funnier— best friend Kyle, I came to the beautiful conclusion that life is one big waggle dance. And that conclusion reframed the way I thought about life. It was the biggest lesson I learned in my hard season.

Instead of worrying about being perfect, planning every detail, or hanging on to guilt, shame, and insecurity, I learned how much more powerful it is to experience, learn, and, of course, survive. Most importantly, I learned how powerful it is to use what you have learned, in all seasons, to help others if you can.

But here comes the most important and purposeful part: The truth is, everyone can create their own waggle dance. Including you.

Everyone can create their own waggle dance because, simply put, life happens to all of us. Like the old phrase goes, "you live and you learn." Like a bee, creating a waggle dance means sharing your invaluable information to help and guide others in a meaningful way that humbly but confidently whispers, *"I've been there too."*

I wrote this book because I believe hard seasons are our best teachers, and what we learn should be used to help others. But I believe that *all* seasons have something to offer. Unfortunately, I think sometimes there is a misconception out there that you need a life-altering event or catastrophic encounter to learn a lesson worth sharing. I do not believe that is true. I hope that you will see in my story that even everyday encounters or common life endeavors can result in stories and lessons worth sharing.

On the other hand, some of us spend an obnoxious, and perhaps debilitating, amount of time trying to analyze ourselves and the lives we are living. I think the waggle dance will help with that too. By the end of this book, I hope you can look at your own life and start to connect the dots, if not for yourself then perhaps for someone you love.

Because a waggle dance uses our less-than-perfect, hard-earned knowledge and unique authenticity to be a funnel for good.

If you are not quite there with me yet, my hope is that you will be soon. Because I can tell you one thing with certainty: I believe that God places people in your life for a reason, and I am beyond grateful for the people in my life and the wisdom they have shared with me. At the very least, this is a book inspired by and dedicated to those people and all the talks and moments we have shared.

The book is divided into three parts: Your *hive*, the goodness and the people that surround you. Your *stings*, the sometimes inevitable difficult circumstances in life.

And finally your *flight*, the moment in your life where you decide how you want to live and be known. Each chapter will share a short story about a time in my life and the discovery I made during that time, which was drawn together by faith, friendship, and everything in between. My stories are not necessarily told in chronological order, and they are only as accurate as memory allows. But they are real and they are mine. This is my honest and best guess of how to connect the dots of my life and what I learned from doing so. It's my "I've been there too" moment for you, wherever and whenever you may find it.

Most importantly, it is my own little waggle dance for my son, "Little Bee." At the end of each chapter, you will find a letter written to him. When I wrote these letters, I often would close my eyes and picture them as a conversation between him and me. I thought about what I would want him to know about my life and, more importantly, the people in it. I thought about what I would want to tell him if he ever experienced similar situations to the ones I experienced. If there ever comes a day when I am not on this earth to tell him these things myself, I will be at peace knowing I have left my stories and heart on these pages for him. My hope is that this book always finds him—and you—in the moments where you may need a little waggle-dancing friend.

Thanks, Kyle, and thank you all for going on this journey with me.

PART ONE

YOUR HIVE

1

WHEN YOU'RE IN A HARD SEASON

This Too Shall Pass

In loving memory of Virginia Sukay

Although I knew life without my grandmother was inevitable at some point, like most of us who lose a loved one, I was not prepared to say goodbye when the time came.

It was December 3, 2019, and I had just left a work conference in Detroit. It was a notoriously dark, cold, and rainy Michigan winter night. As I drove back to my hotel that evening in my rented Chevrolet Malibu, I was thinking about my life and the choices I'd made in it. I felt lost. I felt hopeless. I felt ashamed. I was not in the best place mentally or emotionally. At this point in my life, I could no longer ignore the doubts I had about my marriage, and I wondered how much longer I could go on feeling the way I did. I was grieving all the broken promises I had made to myself.

I wanted so badly to talk to my grandmother about this. I needed her advice. She had always been my source of consolation and guidance. I believed she would understand and would know just what to do, but I hadn't yet found the courage or the words to tell her.

And then my phone rang.

On the other end of the line was my mom. She was crying hysterically. And somehow, I already knew. When my mom finally was able to speak, she told me my grandmother was gone. She had died that evening in hospice with my mom and my aunt by her side. My brother had arrived shortly after she'd passed.

I had missed my chance to say goodbye. To tell her I loved her one last time. To hear her tell me she loved me too. To ask her what I should do. I was numb. I was empty.

I immediately pulled my vehicle off the side of the road and called the first person I could think of—my coworker Michael, the man who eventually would become my husband. I sobbed. I told him the news and then quickly hung up. Admittedly, I was initially both shocked and embarrassed by my decision to call him. We had just started working together, and there were several other people that one could argue I should have instinctively called first. But I didn't. I called him.

I think subconsciously I knew that day was coming and was closer than I was prepared for. The last time I had spoken to my grandmother was on her birthday, November 11. The amount of time that had passed since our last call was unusual—we usually talked more frequently—but I hadn't been able to bring myself to call her. I think deep down, I did not want to know what it would feel like if she didn't answer.

Now, I would spend the rest of my life not having to wonder.

My grandmother was my best friend, my always-first phone call and the one person who knew how to make everything okay. She had a wit that would make your jaw drop—sometimes in an uncomfortable and awkward kind of way—rarely turned down a cosmopolitan, and could pull off leopard print better than anyone I knew. Her hair was always done, her lipstick was always on, and she remained insistent that her nails were always polished, right up until the day she died. She was unapologetically opinionated and loved her family fiercely. She was my favorite person.

Growing up, my brother, Ryan, and I spent a lot of time with our grandmother, who we referred to as "Grammy," or even "Gig." Admittedly, at first I'd found her to be a strict and unforgiving woman. I wasn't at all like her; instead, I favored my grandfather. But as the years went by, my perspective changed drastically and my relationship with Grammy grew stronger and stronger. If you were to ask me why this change occurred, I could not tell you. But what I can tell you is my life was forever changed for the better because of this woman.

I have so many memories of Grammy picking me up from school, taking me shopping, and driving me to work. I even have memories of stealing the red and purple Skittles she kept in a crystal jar on an end table in the living room. Growing up, some of my best days were the Fridays when she would get her hair done at the local shopping mall and take me to the toy store to pick out a puzzle. Never a flashy toy or the newest Barbie. Just a puzzle.

I remember the day she discovered I had a tattoo, and how I tried to convince her it was only a temporary one until she proceeded to chase me around the kitchen trying to wipe it off with her finger. And I still remember the times when I would leave my internship at lunch, go to her apartment, and sit with her while we ate and watched *Criminal Minds* together. She had the biggest crush on Shemar Moore.

Although Grammy has been physically gone from this earth for several years now, I still remember how soft her hands felt when I would hold them in church, or how big her smile was when I'd randomly show up at her doorstep just to hug her in the middle of the afternoon.

To this day, I still catch myself picking up the phone to call her, just to hear her voice.

In the days that preceded her funeral, I was asked by my aunt Missy to give Grammy's eulogy. This task sent me into a whirlwind of memories and introspection. My grandmother had given me so much in life, but I needed her now more than ever—and she had left me.

I struggled to find the words to say. How could I come up with anything that could explain, or give honor to, the woman who had meant so much in my life?

And then I realized that what I needed, she had already given me. Time and time again. So, trusting this truth, I started to write.

> *This too shall pass.*
>
> *It's a phrase that I have no doubt has been shared and trusted by many, and, if you search its origin, you will find a variety of conclusions and explanations. It's a phrase that allows many of us to find comfort in the fact that hardships in life will come to pass. And a reminder for us to enjoy the things in life that we don't want to come to pass, but inevitably do.*
>
> *This too shall pass—it is one of the many things that my grandmother, Virginia Sukay, taught me.*

On the day of her funeral, I gave this eulogy standing in front of her casket, in my own leopard print jacket with tear-filled eyes and an empty yet full heart.

My grandmother—who lived to be ninety-three—always found a way to remind me that "this too shall pass," with a loving and reassuring confidence in her tone that made it impossible to doubt. Even when something difficult was happening in my life and I was struggling to make my way through it, like the time my mom went through a divorce and I was afraid for her and for us, my grandmother was there to remind me, "This too shall pass." With every setback, she encouraged me to remember that hard times don't last. That eventually, they do end and we move forward, typically stronger because of them.

Grammy also kindly reminded me that "this too shall pass" whenever we experienced life's joys, like the mornings after my mom had left for work and we put a puzzle together over slices of her famous cinnamon-buttered toast. I didn't realize then how quickly life would move, or how much I would miss those mornings spent together.

But I have since learned that not a single moment can remain forever, no matter how badly we wish it could.

It wasn't until writing her eulogy that I fully appreciated how much *this too shall pass* became my life mantra. Not just during difficulties, but also as a constant reminder that everything we experience in our lifetime is painfully temporary.

And that is when I realized that while I may not be able to pick up the phone and talk to her, she had already given me all the advice I needed before she physically left this earth. Her words had left an undeniable impression on my heart and given me the ground I needed to stand on. She was both gone and standing right there with me.

In the months that followed my grandmother's passing, I knew my divorce was inevitable. But I also knew I would be okay. Because she'd raised me to believe, and to trust, that *this too shall pass*.

Her words also became my promise to begin to live life more intentionally. I knew that the best way to honor her life would be to appreciate the people and experiences placed in my path and to take them for all they were worth. Some of this came to me as hindsight; some of it had only just begun.

This promise is one that continues to this very day with me and my husband, Michael. In our home we refrain from saying "I can't wait," for this very reason. It may sound silly and simple, but the truth is we believe we *can* wait—and we *want* to wait—because, like my grandmother promised, *this too shall pass*. Michael and I are committed to waiting for what God is bringing next, so that we can fully enjoy and experience what He is giving us now.

My grandmother may not be here with me in the physical sense, but I believe she actually is here. She will always be here. That's because my grandmother lives in the deepest part of my soul. Maybe that is why I never had the chance to tell her goodbye.

My grandmother taught me how to pick my battles—and how to win them. She taught me how to say what you mean and mean what you say, and she taught me that the ability to backpedal can sometimes be very useful.

She taught me strength, she taught me kindness.

My grandmother taught me that *this too shall pass.*

Thank you, Grammy.

Dear Little Bee,

You have no idea how badly I wish you could have met your great-grandmother while she was here on earth. But there hasn't been a day since you were born where I haven't thought of her and the wisdom she shared. My prayer is that by knowing me, you will also know her.

There will be days or seasons in your life when it feels like there is no end or reprieve in sight. These times may seem impossibly difficult, but I promise, you will be okay. This too shall pass.

There will also undoubtedly be times in your life when you find yourself anxiously awaiting whatever comes next, and in your fruitless pursuit of answers, you might miss the magic happening right before your eyes. Like the feeling of your own child wrapping their arms around your neck, or the joy of being hugged by someone you love.

Finally, and thankfully, there will be a lot of moments that overflow your joy bucket. I want you to swim in the water of joy as much as you can. Pay attention to every detail and every feeling that bubbles up. Do not waste your joy. And please resist the urge to rush to get something done; just enjoy your moment. Because like it or not, this too shall pass.

Please trust me that there is no day that is too small or too unimportant. Every single day is a gift, regardless of the struggle, anxiety, or joy you find in it.

Eventually, life becomes a collection of memories. We never know when our last memory will be made, so I will always pray that you make your days count.

And Little Bee, please know that the relationships you have with your grandparents are beyond special and should not be taken for granted. Pick up the phone and call them, often. Or, better yet, go visit them. I promise you that every minute you spend with them will be one you cherish for the rest of your life.

Never pass up the chance to tell someone you love them.

Little Bee, I love you so much.

Verses for When You're in a Hard Season

For our present troubles are small and won't last very long. Yet they produce for us a glory that vastly outweighs them and will last forever! (2 Corinthians 4:17 NLT)

So be truly glad. There is wonderful joy ahead, even though you must endure trials for a little while. (1 Peter 1:6 NLT)

Questions for When You're in a Hard Season

- What is one of the hardest things you have ever been through?
- What did that experience teach you?
- What would you tell someone else going through something similar?
- What do you want your family to say for your eulogy?

Now, are you ready to dance?

2

WHEN YOU FEEL INFERIOR

Learn Something from Everyone You Meet

I was in my early twenties when I walked through the large glass doors of one of Detroit's largest automakers for the very first time. After graduating from a small state school, Slippery Rock University of Pennsylvania, with a bachelor's degree in communications, I accepted a prestigious internship position with the auto giant General Motors, moved to Detroit, and soon was regularly wiping the sweat off my palms before shaking the hands of strangers who would eventually become colleagues and friends.

For starters, the only thing I really knew about cars was what my dad and brother, Ryan, attempted to teach me in our garage at home while I was growing up. Which, thankfully, turns out was actually quite a bit. But truthfully, I was still nervous. Not just the normal jitters we all typically feel when we start new things, but the kind that kept me up at night. The kind that made me struggle to regulate my thoughts in an attempt to spit out complete sentences. The kind that left me going home every day replaying over and over in my head the conversations and interactions I'd had that workday, trying to evaluate how I'd done.

As I continued to endure those sweaty-awkward handshakes and introductions in the months to come, I could not help but feel totally out of my league. Here I was, a small-town girl from Pennsylvania who'd suddenly begun to doubt every qualification and accomplishment she'd ever had.

This. Was. The. Big. Leagues.

But I was desperate. Desperate to prove my worth and earn my seat at the table. I remember thinking that maybe if I could fool my colleagues into believing I belonged there, I could actually learn enough to emulate the excellence I was surrounded by.

For context, Ryan and I grew up in a modest household with our mom, who showed us what hard work really looked like. I do not remember many times when she was not working more than one job in order to provide for her children and the dreams we had. And the same goes for my dad. A simple and uncomplicated man by nature, he worked hard and saved harder. My parents divorced when I was a baby, yet I still consider myself very loved and very lucky. Because of the love my parents and our entire family showed me, I do not remember wanting for anything as a child, but as I grew older, the truth is—I did want more.

I wanted the kind of home that came with both a mom and a dad under the same roof. A home that was filled with family movie nights, church on Sundays, and evenings spent around the dinner table. I wanted to unhear the financial struggles my mom constantly talked about and the worries she voiced aloud about making ends meet or finding someone to spend her life with. I wanted something easier and more stable. I will always credit Mom for teaching me the value of hard work, but I knew in my heart there had to be a better way to live my life.

So here I was, over twenty years later, with what felt like a chance to make it happen in this new, corporate automotive world—and I was completely terrified to fail. But maybe fear was my motivator, because I worked harder than I ever had before.

After a relatively short but impactful summer as an intern, I was offered a full-time position with General Motors. My family was proud of me, and I was getting closer to being able to provide for myself—and for my future family—in the way I'd always envisioned. I firmly believed that a well-paying, steady job was the first step to living a successful life.

Yet even after I received the full-time offer, my confidence did not immediately make an appearance. Instead, it stayed hidden under layers of insecurities and doubts. In so many ways, I still did not believe I deserved to be there. I remember several meetings where I would be sitting around the table in a conference room and, rather than contribute, I simply listened in awe. I was in awe of the ideas and knowledge of the people surrounding me. Hell, I was in awe of just their vocabulary. It was almost impossible to feel like I could hold my own in these conference rooms. What original ideas or thoughts could I have that these people didn't?

The next few years were filled with more self-doubt and consistent feedback telling me I needed to start speaking up more. I was doing well enough to get by, but inside I was swirling in a cloud of confusion. The girl I'd been in Pennsylvania was confident, sure of herself, on top of her game. This new version of me was self-critical, more anxious than ever, and, more often than not, completely doubting what she was capable of.

But then, with the help of a dear friend and irreplaceable mentor, I reached a turning point.

Early in my career, I worked for a leader named Mike, who I have since affectionately nicknamed "Boss." Mike was someone who I began to truly trust and build a relationship with. He had been with the company for several years and had an ease and familiarity about him that both drew me in and disarmed me. Originally from the East Coast, he was sarcastic, funny, and incredibly straightforward. There was no corporate fluff about Mike, and I loved that. Within the four walls of his office, we had countless moving and meaningful conversations. Some about work, most about life—but, like his personality, always completely casual and honest in nature.

Every morning, before most of our team started their day, I would badge in, black backpack in tow, take one of the four glass elevators to the thirtieth floor, and walk past the big glass windows in Mike's office, waving good morning to him. Then, less than ten minutes later—after I'd responded to emails and organized my day—I would find myself knocking on his door, asking if he was busy, already knowing he would lie and tell me no. I would plop myself down on a leather chair next to a very odd and undoubtedly outdated lava lamp. And we'd begin talking. It was my favorite part of the day, every day.

It was in one of these seemingly ordinary conversations that Mike looked over the edge of his dark-rimmed glasses, took a sip of coffee, and shared a piece of wisdom with me that changed the trajectory of how I viewed the world around me.

"The truth is, you can learn something from everyone you meet."

In the moment it was a simple, almost obvious, piece of advice given to no doubt help calm my nerves. In fact, I am quite certain Mike has long since forgotten he even said those words to me. But they immediately changed how I viewed those tables I was sitting at, and, without me even realizing it, I began to fundamentally change the way I approached life. Instead of trying to prove to everyone that I deserved to be there, or worrying about what I could contribute or how I would be perceived, I shifted my focus to searching for what I could learn from the people around me.

And it worked. Turns out, you can learn quite a bit when you approach situations in this way. At first, it was little things—like the way my colleagues phrased thoughts and presented ideas. Or, admittedly, the fancy words they used. But I also studied their body language to try and learn more about them and how they navigated different dynamics. They were not trying to, but they were absolutely teaching me with every encounter.

There was a lot to admire, and certainly a lot to learn. Just as important in those early learnings were the qualities I didn't particularly care for or want to emulate. For instance, I didn't love the harshness of some colleagues, or the way others seemed to thrive in the quiet whispers shared behind their peers' backs. Having been on the receiving end of both, I'll state the obvious—it hurt. A lot.

However, as it turns out, the hurt was quite a powerful learning opportunity. In fact, I think that is part of what Mike was trying to tell me that day: even a bad interaction with someone is teaching us something, even if it's just how *not* to act.

As I started to approach life like this—specifically, my professional life—I found my mind to be more at ease. I was starting to take the pressure off myself. Little by little, I began to open up. I was learning more than ever, and I was gaining confidence along the way. The less of a front I put up, the more of a sponge I became.

One of the first and greatest lessons I learned was the power of authenticity. I realized that the people I was most drawn to, like my mentors Monte and Leslie, were unapologetically themselves. Monte was my internship supervisor, and he was always the jokester in the room with creative ideas and big stories. He had a natural ability to solve complex problems with simple solutions, and never once do I remember seeing him worried or worked up over the stress of his job. Leslie was an organized and caring leader who was never afraid to lead with her heart and let you know how much she cared. When I was new to the team, she went out of her way to teach me and help me.

Mike, Monte, and Leslie instantly made this big company feel like home to me. None of them ever tried to be the smartest person in the room, and they certainly did not appear to be worried about what other people thought about them. They were just themselves. Yet, in my opinion, they are some of the most intelligent and well-respected people I've ever worked with. Likely without knowing it, Mike, Monte, and Leslie began to give me permission to be myself and to trust that I could do this.

As the years went by, I took on several new assignments within the company. Each time, I battled feelings of insecurity. It's hard to understand why, but I have recognized that as a default feeling of mine. Whenever I find myself in new and unfamiliar territory, if I am not careful, I can revert to the girl who doubts her every qualification. Who, rather than starting with a learner attitude and from a place of confidence, wastes time second-guessing her instincts, her experience, and just about everything in between. I stumble over my words, stay quiet when I have an opinion, and spend hours agonizing over how I'm being perceived.

But recognizing this about myself is a powerful tool, because with awareness comes the ability to redirect those negative thoughts. And the ability to redirect comes solely from experience and self-given confidence. Now, whenever I find myself in a moment of inferiority, I try to remember the advice given and examples shown to me by Mike, Monte, and Leslie. In any moment of doubt, I do my best to just trust myself. If I am unsure about something, rather than feeling insecure about it, I choose to ask about it.

The more I have asked, the more I have learned. And the more I have learned, the more confidence I have found. Eventually, I realized that people had something to learn from me too. And that is important because, like another great mentor, Kim, once shared with me, sometimes you need to know when to ask a question and when to make a statement. It has been both amazing and rewarding to find myself in a place with more statements than questions, but remembering to stay grounded in the humility of continuing to ask questions. The more you are yourself and the more questions you ask, the more confidence you will acquire and the stronger your statements will be.

Thank you to Mike, Monte, Leslie, and Kim.

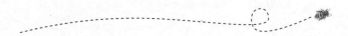

Dear Little Bee,

It is inevitable that you will find yourself in new and challenging opportunities in this lifetime. Despite my best attempts to tell you otherwise, your natural instinct might be to question your worth or your ability to succeed in those moments.

So, try this instead. Rather than focusing on yourself, I want you to focus more on the world around you. As you turn your attention outward, you will quickly realize that you are surrounded by all different types of people. Regardless of your personal opinions of them, you can learn something from each and every person.

There will be people who inspire and guide you. There will be people who challenge and frustrate you. Even if you happen not to like them, they all have something to teach you. Never be too proud or insecure to pay attention to what that might be.

The next time you are feeling inferior, don't worry about trying to prove something right away; instead, be humble enough to receive something. Show up early and show up as yourself. Own who you are. I promise—it is someone special.

Ask a lot of questions. Questions are not a sign of weakness or ignorance, but rather a sign of confidence and humility. I believe that questions are the key to unlocking magic. By the way, your dad asks the best ones, even if I frequently tell him he has reached his question limit.

Be ready to look for the moments in which it is time for you to make a statement. There is a place for both listening and speaking in this world, but trust me, you deserve to have your statements heard.

Ultimately, my hope for you, Little Bee, is that you will choose to be a sponge and soak in the world around you. Life is too short to live it passively, and the people in your path are there for a reason. Let them in. Learn from them.

Verses for When You Feel Inferior

Since we have gifts that differ according to the grace given to us, let us exercise them. (Romans 12:6 NABRE)

For just as we have many members in one body and all the members do not have the same function, so we, who are many, are one body in Christ, and individually members of one another. (Romans 12:4–5 NASB1995)

Questions for When You Feel Inferior

- What can you learn from this moment or this person to help you feel more confident in the future?
- How would you know if you never asked?
- What can you teach other people based on what you've learned?

Now let's dance that dance of learning, shall we?

3

WHEN YOU WANT TO
SEE IT DIFFERENTLY

Dream Bigger

I was twenty years old when I realized I'd had enough, in the most first-world problem way ever. I was sick of my small town and the endless drama that came with it, and I had just recently had my ego bruised by the college jock I was dating who'd thought he could get away with it—and who kind of did. I had four months left of my sophomore year of college. For all the reasons stated above and more, in no way could I picture myself returning home for the summer after classes ended. So one day, during my usual shift at the campus camera equipment room, I googled "internships abroad." The internet search results generated, and I started clicking. Thanks to some clever search optimization, the company Dream Careers landed at the top of my page.

Dream Careers sounded interesting. I learned that this program had been established to help students like me find internship opportunities in other countries. Remembering my inability to speak any language other than English, I did a quick scan of available locations until I found one where I would at least be able to read road signs and have a conversation: London. With a target destination in mind, I picked up the phone and called the one person I knew would be on my side: my dad.

"Dad, I want to go work in London this summer instead of coming home."

"Good. Do it," he said. My dad is not a man of many words, but there is something about his tone that leaves little question about where he stands on something.

So back to the website I went. I applied for the position in London and landed an internship with a public relations company in the fashion industry. Four months later, I was packing my bags and saying goodbye to friends and family at an England-themed party my mom hosted in our backyard.

Before I even landed in London, it already felt like I had taken such a big step in my life. It was the longest amount of time I'd ever been away from home, the farthest distance I'd ever traveled, the longest flight I'd ever been on, and one of the only flights I'd ever taken by myself. I felt the distance from what was familiar almost immediately. When I landed in London the next morning, I quickly found transportation and made my way to King's Cross, the location of the apartment building I'd be staying in for the summer.

I still remember opening the door to this small apartment, a room that could not have been bigger than seven feet wide. There was one tiny window, and standing in front of it was one of the most beautiful people I'd ever seen in my life: Demi, my new roommate. The first thing I noticed was this undeniable light and energy coming from her; the second thing I noticed was her hair. *My God, she has the best hair,* I thought to myself.

Demi was originally from Georgia but was currently living in Florida and attending one of the state universities there. We had never met before, yet somehow within moments, we felt like old friends. I quickly learned that she had a deep faith and passion for helping other people, which partly explained the light emulating from her. After we unpacked our things, which had to be creatively stored under our twin beds to save room, it was time to venture out into the city. Riding the high of this newfound adventure, we picked up the necessary supplies at a local mart, including a calling card, a hair dryer, deodorant, and cleaning supplies. With our newly purchased essentials in tow, we made our way back to our shoebox apartment to get ready for the program orientation that evening.

Hours later, we quietly found seats in the back of the room, made a pact not to talk to anyone right away, and waited patiently for the program organizer to make his remarks.

Before we knew it, Demi and I were greeted by one of the most energetic, forward people I have ever met, Chelsea, who from across the room had decided that Demi and I were two people she wanted to meet. Chelsea was from California and was pursuing comedy and acting in Hollywood. I had never, in all my small-town life, met a girl quite like her. She was unapologetically honest, Jewish, and never fell short on opinions or funny punch lines. But her humor and candor were only part of the equation. I later learned that prior to coming to London, Chelsea had lost her dad to amyotrophic lateral sclerosis, commonly referred to as ALS, and that her mom was battling stage four breast cancer.

Today, Chelsea is a grief advocate who uses her gift for and love of comedy to help others normalize grief and process death. This only solidifies my first impression: there is no one else like her.

Chelsea was roommates with Jamie Lin, a tall Taiwanese woman who was born in Taiwan, had lived in Hawaii, and was currently attending school in California. It did not take me long to realize just how incredibly well-traveled and cultured Jamie Lin was, which was impressive given the fact that most of us had barely reached our twenties. Jamie Lin and I struck up an immediate friendship, probably partly because we were the tallest people and the slowest walkers in the group.

And then there was Margaret, or "Marge in Charge," as we quickly and affectionately nicknamed her. Margaret was from New York, and she was familiar to me in all the typical East Coast ways, but unfamiliar in the sense that she was a seemingly perfect blend of authority and gentleness. She was the first to pull up her maps and guide us to wherever we were going, the last to go to bed, and the first to drop breakfast off outside our door the morning after we'd had too much to drink.

Together, we all lived the summer of a lifetime. Within weeks, we became the self-titled Dream Team, and it was a title we took very seriously. All of us had different jobs and we worked hard-ish at those jobs eight to nine hours a day, five days a week. Afterward, we ate a cheap dinner and had a late night filled with adventure and never-before-experienced moments—like the time we stayed out until 4 a.m. to celebrate the Fourth of July in the very country that we celebrated our separation from.

We also traveled to Paris and ate crepes just a stone's throw away from the Eiffel Tower. We walked for hours around Hyde Park and met people from all across the world. We went to Brighton and had tea with locals, who Chelsea somehow knew. And later we visited Stonehenge, a place I'd only ever seen in movies.

But for me, perhaps the most significant experience was that it was the first time my eyes were opened to the idea that my circle will only stay as small as I let it. Before I met these women, I'd spent the majority of my life surrounded by like-minded and like-experienced people. I'd never ventured very far away from home. And while there can be value in that, I quickly learned what is possible when you dream your circle just a little bit bigger.

In hindsight, I knew I was going "across the pond," but I had absolutely no idea how big the ocean was. London was an experience I never thought would be possible for someone like me. I was in a new world, surrounded by inspiring and fierce women, and the end result was that it left me craving more. I wanted to see more, do more, learn more, and I hoped to do all of the above with people like these women. For the first time in my life, I realized just how much there was to experience and how capable I was to go out and experience it.

The months flew by and before we knew it, it was time for all of us to go back home. I remember struggling with the idea that I had to return to what had been at one time so familiar. But it was inevitable. We repacked our bags, said our tearful goodbyes, promised to see one another soon, and then off we went.

On an early morning cab ride to London Heathrow airport, I realized that while we'd all come to London for different reasons, we were all leaving with a gift we'd never seen coming: the gift of each other.

That was more than ten years ago. Under so many normal circumstances, these friendships would have dissolved by now. But it was clear, just like our backgrounds and journeys, that our relationships were different. These women are still some of the greatest friends I have in my life today.

Since our time together in London, this unexpected group of friends has visited more than seven states together. We have been at each other's weddings, slept in each other's childhood bedrooms, and shared more bottles of wine than I care to admit.

Recently, Demi, Chelsea, Jamie Lin, and Margaret traveled to Missouri to meet my newborn son. They surprised me by booking a trip that was coordinated through my husband. The significance of all of them dropping what they were doing, booking a flight, and spending the weekend in our home—because they wanted to meet my family—was not lost on me.

During one night of their visit, we all went out to dinner. It was normal for us to share good meals, good drinks, and even better conversations. But this one felt different.

We were sitting around a wooden table, tucked quietly in the corner of a small restaurant in downtown Kansas City, and we were talking about the usual deep topics like marriage and family. But we were also talking about our dreams. Dreams about our careers, about ourselves, and even, on some level, about the world around us. As we took turns sharing our perspective and experience, I was reminded of just how different we all truly were. Somewhere in the middle of a decade, I'd lost sight of that fact, probably because we had grown so close and shared so many beautiful moments together.

As I was reminded of our differences, at first I had a hard time processing it. In some ways I felt less-than and insecure; in other ways I felt reinvigorated.

It took me a minute, but then I came right back to the place where it had all started—the place where I realized how amazing it was to be surrounded by four women who saw and experienced the world very differently than me. Their existence once again opened my eyes to all there is in life to experience.

With a heart full of gratitude, I once again began to appreciate how these differences kept expanding my circle, even after years of established friendships. Here these women were, more than ten years later, still challenging me to think differently about opinions I had once held so strongly. Like they had in so many of our previous powerful conversations, these friends made me take a step back and consider a larger picture—a picture that had many different vantage points.

In so many worlds, differences can keep us apart. But in my world, these differences only made my circle bigger. These friendships have been my constant reminder that if we are not careful, our circles, viewpoints, and lives can become very small. The challenge is to keep dreaming bigger. To fill your circle to what might feel like its breaking point, only then to be held together by an unbreakable bond.

Thank you, to my Dream Team.

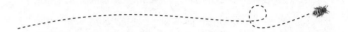

Dear Little Bee,

I will likely never be ready for the day where you tell me you are ready to spread your wings. I can only guess that it will go against every internal narrative and instinct I have. But when that point comes, I promise to do my best to let you go. I promise to help you find confidence in your choice, just like your Pap did for me.

And when you go, wherever you land, I will pray that you find yourself surrounded by people from all different corners of this world. People who, with every conversation, expand your circle just a little bit bigger.

In life, we sometimes shy away from things that scare, intimidate, or challenge us, and we stay where it feels safe and comfortable. But I want you to be the kind of person who steps confidently forward and embraces that healthy opposition. If you want to go experience something, do it. You have what it takes, and I have your back. While the path ahead of you may not be clear, God's plan for you is good. More on that later.

Filling your circle with unique friendships is a must. It does and will require constant intentionality on your part, but I promise it is worth it. Find friendships that will outlast distance, differences, and all seasons of life.

And just because you are blessed enough to have friends in your life for decades does not mean you still can't learn something new about them. Never stop getting to know the people who fill your circle.

Verses for When You Want to See It Differently

Trust in the LORD with all your heart and lean not on your own understanding; in all your ways submit to him, and he will make your paths straight. (Proverbs 3:5–6 NIV)

Have I not commanded you? Be strong and courageous. Do not be afraid, do not be discouraged, for the LORD your God will be with you wherever you go. (Joshua 1:9 NIV)

Questions for When You Want to See It Differently

- What can you learn from this different perspective?
- How can you expose yourself to new experiences and new people?
- What would happen if you tried this new thing or went to this new place?

Dance that dance of possibilities.

4

WHEN YOU WANT CONNECTION

Everyone Has a Story to Share . . . Including You

In loving memory of Christian Cooper

Like most eager college students, I spent most of my summers working various internships and jobs to build a strong résumé and to help put gas in my car. One of my first internships gave me the opportunity to live with family just outside of Pittsburgh, working in communications for a well-known golf league. I can't say I knew much about golf, but I was intrigued by the idea of working in the sports industry and excited about the opportunity to live with my aunt Missy and uncle Bernie for a few months.

Growing up, I was always incredibly close with them. My mom and dad chose them as my godparents and, because of that and my proximity to them both, our relationship only strengthened as the years went on. Aunt Missy and Uncle Bernie treated me like their own daughter and always took a great deal of interest in me and my future. It is something I still thank them for to this day.

I liked my internship well enough that summer, but the best part was that during most evenings, after the rest of the family had gone to bed, Uncle Bernie would convince me to stay up just a little longer, make us a cocktail—usually a vodka-cranberry—and we'd head outside and sit next to the fireplace and talk for what felt like hours.

Our talks were almost always led by Uncle Bernie's ability to ask questions. I loved this about him—how the way he asked the questions always made me feel like he cared and was listening. His questions made me feel like I had a place and a purpose.

And that is only one of the qualities I admire about my uncle Bernie. He also has a natural ability to put anyone at ease and make them feel like they're the most important person in the room. People are drawn to him, and understandably so. Some would say that is how he made such a successful career for himself in sales, but I think it goes deeper than that. I believe it's more about who he is than what he does. Who he is extends much further than his ability to have a conversation and make a sale. A man of faith and family, Uncle Bernie gave me a front-row seat that allowed me to see the kind of family and legacy I wanted for myself.

I have thought a lot about those late-night conversations on my aunt and uncle's back porch. At the time, they felt like a fun way to end the evening. But in hindsight, I've realized just how much they have shaped my life. Because without those conversations, I am not sure I would have known how to ask questions and listen the way I do today. Or maybe I just would not have valued that type of communication as much. Either way, I am positive that without that love, support, and ongoing conversation, my life would not have been filled with moments like this next one I'm going to tell you about.

It was several years later and early in my career when I was given the opportunity to support a media drive for automotive journalists in San Francisco, California. Media drives are curated opportunities for members of the media to drive vehicles before they are made available to customers, with the hope that the journalists will write pieces sharing positive impressions and stories based on their experience. I remember this particular event like it was yesterday. It was the first time I'd ever rented a car by myself, the first time I'd driven on a six-lane highway, and the first time in my life I'd seen the Golden Gate Bridge. But what stands out most in my mind is that it was also perhaps the first time I became acutely aware of just how rushed I was to get things done and what I might miss as a result.

On an early fall afternoon, our internal team was on-site getting everything ready for the following day for when our media guests would arrive. The best way I can describe this moment was expensive organized chaos at its finest. The event structures were being built by a hired production crew right before my eyes, and cars were being loaded in with trucks and cranes. The staff was preparing three-course meals and the subject matter experts were being briefed and trained nearby. It was amazing to watch and somewhat surreal to be a part of.

I quickly learned that as a member of the communications team, you often find yourself in an orchestrator-like position during these events. It is your job to know who is doing what, when they are doing it, and what they need to have to be successful.

For this particular media program, I was trusted with responsibilities that often included making a list and checking it twice—so that is exactly what I did. I was also there to watch and to learn, and to hopefully begin to develop relationships that would become critical to my success throughout the years.

List in hand, I remember walking up a notoriously steep San Francisco hill that day as the finishing touches were being made in our event space. Hair pulled back and Chevrolet-branded clothing worn proudly, I was a woman on a mission. I was also a woman who was pretending to know what she was doing half the time and praying that no one noticed she actually had no idea. As I crested the top of the hill, I noticed that seated just near the entrance to the event space was a gentleman I'd never met before. He was quietly sitting alone, nose buried in one of the notebooks we'd handed out to our design and engineering team members. He seemed so peaceful.

I had every intention of quickly waving and walking past him so I could continue doing my job, but he looked up at me with one of the most welcoming and genuine smiles I'd ever seen, said hello, and introduced himself as Stuart, a member of our vehicle design team. He had an amazing English accent and an instant warmth about him. Before I knew it, we weren't just exchanging pleasantries, but we were telling each other our life stories. I forgot all about the things I needed to get done. Chatting with Stuart, I learned that he and his wife and their two children had moved to the US from England with aspirations of receiving better healthcare for their son, Christian. I learned that he loved my favorite sports team (go Steelers!) and a good cup of coffee just as much as I did. It is hard to explain the joy I felt after that conversation with Stuart, but there was an undeniable light and calmness that he brought to my heart within minutes of getting to know him. Our conversation that day reminded me that while getting things done and checking off tasks on a to-do list certainly feels good, it isn't nearly as good as the feeling of truly connecting with another person. I would have missed getting to know Stuart had I not slowed down long enough to listen.

After our conversation, I proceeded into the event space and looked at the electric vehicle parked right in the center of the room. Under an intense spotlight, no longer was I just staring at sheets of cobalt blue metal—instead, I was looking at artwork that had come from the mind of my new friend, Stuart. And that notebook he was sketching in? It is on my desk nearly ten years later. In an almost-missed moment, Stuart taught me that people have stories worth hearing; we just have to slow down long enough to listen to them.

Life might move fast, but we don't always have to.

The decision to slow down that day reminded me what I believe life is all about: each other, and our ability to listen to the stories all around us. I have reflected on my encounter with Stuart a lot over the past few years and what our friendship has brought to my life. After I met Stuart, I became more fascinated with other people's stories—who they were and why they were the way they were, what they were doing and why they were doing it. It is safe to say that this moment in my career lit a fire of curiosity within me that continues to be fueled by the people I meet.

Yet as much as I loved knowing and ultimately sharing other people's stories, I spent years hiding my own. Especially after my divorce.

The thought of someday sharing parts of my own story felt downright scary. My career was built around storytelling and public perception, and I think that as a result, I only wanted to share the good parts of my own story with other people. I wanted ultimate control of the narrative. But through a series of experiences, I learned that our most authentic and vulnerable stories are often the most powerful ones. I learned that sometimes, by sharing your own story, you can connect with and help someone else.

In early 2020 I had the opportunity to work with two women named Rita and Sheila. I did not know either of them very well before we started working together, but over time we built a close friendship. Rita was a mother of three and a devout Catholic, and Sheila was a well-known and respected leader who also prioritized her family and faith above everything else.

On the surface, we had little in common. All three of us worked different jobs, came from relatively different backgrounds, and were definitely at different places in our lives. Sheila and Rita each were married and had established families. I was fresh out of a divorce and doing my best to begin again. They were solid in their faith, and I was still reserved and intimidated by spiritual matters. Yet I knew from the start that this was a special friendship, because despite our differences, our friendship quickly became centered around faith, which was an anchor that felt completely unique and special to me in the workplace.

During one of our many meetings together, somewhere in the middle of impending deadlines, key message documents, and deep conversations about religion, Sheila opened up even further and shared some of her life story with us. Much to my surprise, she, too, had gone through a divorce. I remember being in awe that someone like her would have been divorced and would be so open about it.

During this time of my life, I was reluctant to be vulnerable, and I rarely shared details of my divorce or newly formed relationship with Michael, for fear of judgment. Ironically, I was most reserved around women of faith, and at first Rita and Sheila were no exception. But I felt in my heart that these women were a safe place. And they were. Sheila's own vulnerability felt like an invitation to my own. Finally, after months of concealment, I decided to share my experience with them.

This brief but powerful conversation brought us closer and left me feeling lighter. It was a moment in which I realized that so many powerful and beautiful women had been exactly where I stood now. I had taken a first step. A baby step. A meaningful step. And one of the most beautiful results of my decision to share was when, several months later, Rita reached out to me and asked if I would be willing to talk to a friend of hers who was also going through a divorce. Without hesitation, my answer was yes. Like Sheila, I knew it was my time to offer someone else a part of my story as a lifeline. It was a small way for me to pay it forward and to help, similar to the way so many others had helped me. Suddenly, I wasn't as keen on hiding my story anymore.

Two years later, Michael and I moved from Nashville, Tennessee, to Kansas City, Missouri. And, like any other strong woman who had her priorities straight, one of the first orders of business was to find myself a new hairstylist.

On the sacred day of my four-hour hair appointment, I climbed the steep stairs to a second-floor studio and was greeted by Paige, my new stylist. We small-talked for a minute as she buried my hair under mounds of foil, and then one thing led to another. Before I knew it, we were diving into the depths of our souls. She was sharing pieces of her history with me, and in return I was sharing with her.

Paige was a single mom in her twenties who had finally found her forever love, and I was a newly divorced and remarried woman who was about to become a mom. Neither of our stories had perfection, but they had something better—connection. It was the first real conversation I'd had with someone in Kansas City since moving there, and it felt really good and natural.

After we both realized what had just been shared and the feelings that exchange had elicited, we talked about how so many of us are hesitant to share our stories—or at least some parts of them—because we are ultimately afraid of what people might think. And that is a real thing. But the truth is, our stories are powerful and they are needed. That's because our stories are the connective tissue in this world. When we share them, we create opportunities to better connect with those around us. Our stories can be the source of someone else's hope or inspiration. They can be the common ground that gives another person a safe place on which to stand. By sharing our stories, we can let others know they are not alone, and that we, too, have been where they are. But first, we have to stop and listen.

Thank you, Uncle Bernie, Stuart, Rita, Sheila, and Paige.

Dear Little Bee,

I pray that you will be the kind of person who makes others feel seen, and like they have a place and a purpose.

I pray that you will slow down long enough to ask and to listen.

Your never-ending to-do lists will always be there. There will always be something else that needs to get done or somewhere else you need to go. But there may not always be an opportunity to form a new connection or to build a meaningful relationship.

If we are not careful, we can miss these opportunities. But if we are intentional with our time, these moments can enrich our lives and the lives of those around us.

Those slow-down moments are your chance to show humility and empathy and, most importantly, love. The relationships we build throughout our lives are critical. They have the ability to shape us and define us, and they are ultimately how we will be remembered.

I pray that you will find joy in people and their stories.

And as your own story takes shape and continues to evolve, remember that certain seasons of your life are only chapters. They do not define you, but they can help build you and those around you.

You never know how your story can help someone else. You never know who might be able to relate to your experience. The only way of figuring that out is to find the courage to share. Be brave, but be judicious. Not everyone will deserve to hear your story. Do your best to trust your gut and follow your heart—you will know.

Throughout your life you will encounter people who you'll instantly have a connection with. If you're lucky, before you know it you will be sharing life stories and debating some of life's biggest questions together. When this happens, you might agree that this type of connection feels nothing short of magical.

*So be on the lookout for that magical energy that ener-
gizes your heart and instantly makes you feel connected to
someone. And when you find it, Little Bee, trust it.*

Verses for When You Want Connection

You are the light of the world. A city set on a mountain cannot
be hidden. . . . Just so, your light must shine before others,
that they may see your good deeds and glorify your heavenly
Father. (Matthew 5:14, 16 NABRE)

Blessed be the God and Father of our Lord Jesus Christ, the
Father of compassion and God of all encouragement, who
encourages us in our every affliction, so that we may be able
to encourage those who are in any affliction with the encouragement with which we ourselves are encouraged by God.
(2 Corinthians 1:3–4 NABRE)

Keep on doing what you have learned and received and heard
and seen in me. Then the God of peace will be with you. (Philippians 4:9 NABRE)

Questions for When You Want Connection

- If you are in a rush to get something done, can it wait?
- What is the worst thing that could happen by sharing
  your story?

- How does it feel when you learn that someone has been through what you are going through now?
- How can you use the things you have experienced to help someone else?

Inspiration for When You Want Connection

"Vulnerability is not winning or losing; it's having the courage to show up and be seen when we have no control over the outcome. Vulnerability is not weakness; it's our greatest measure of courage." —Brene Brown (adapted from an Instagram post)

Dance your dance vulnerably.

5

WHEN YOU'RE LOOKING FOR MEANING

Don't Mistake "Obvious" for "Meaningless"

My dad was born in Latrobe, Pennsylvania, to Kenneth and Lora Joyce. He grew up in a very small home with his two sisters, Lisa and Lori. He came from extremely humble beginnings, and that humble start to life only followed him throughout the next several decades.

Unlike with my mom's side of our family, I did not know my dad's side well. That is partly because my dad's father died before I was born, and his mom passed away when I was only two months old. Fortunately, I did know one of his two sisters and often spent time with her during holidays. But aside from those infrequent visits, that was it.

As you know, my parents divorced when I was a baby. My dad and stepmother were officially together almost instantly, and, as you can imagine, that was a very interesting and challenging dynamic for everyone. Except for me because, remember—I was only a baby. Sometimes ignorance really is bliss.

One of the results of my parents' divorce was that my brother and I spent the majority of our childhood visiting our dad and stepmother every other weekend and once during the week. Even though I have plenty of childhood memories of my dad, that type of arrangement naturally makes it more challenging to get to know a parent.

But allow me to start with this: different and divorced does not always mean broken.

When you grow up with divorced parents, I think it's easy to focus on all the things you think you missed out on, like never knowing what it was like to wake up with both your mom and your dad in the same house. Or wondering what it would have been like had they never separated to begin with. I also think it's really easy to make assumptions and judgments based on what you perceive has been stolen from you because of your parents' divorce.

I think all of this because yes, I have thought it all.

But the older I got, the more I realized the truth that I did not miss out on anything. And I certainly never felt like a victim of theft. For instance, I don't remember ever being upset about having to spend Christmas or birthdays separate from one of my parents; I viewed it as the chance to celebrate twice. Better than that, I never felt like I had to choose between either parent, and I certainly cannot recall any major life events in which I did not have the support of my mom, dad, and stepmother.

Of course, parenting kids through divorce did not come easily or naturally. And that is why I give the three of them—my mom, dad, and stepmother—a lot of credit. It definitely was not flawless, but they made it work. Somehow, in the middle of separation, disagreements, tension, and less-than-normal circumstances, my parents figured out how to be the best they could be for me, my brother, and now, my son. Of all the things I respect about my parents, that is at the top of my list.

Admittedly, because of our situation, I think it took me much longer to get to know my dad and definitely my stepmother. My dad and brother had natural connection points, like dirt bikes, cars, and hunting. But for me, as a little girl, it was slightly different. I wanted to ride horses, play with Barbies, and have someone do my hair. Needless to say, none of these activities were my dad's specialty.

Eventually, I started to want to do the things that Dad and my brother, Ryan, were doing, like quad riding and fishing. Probably because I wanted more attention from my dad, but also definitely because I took great pleasure in infringing on Ryan's territory and beating him at whatever I could. In fact, some of my dad's favorite stories involve us fishing in New York or me working feverishly to learn how to operate the manual transmission in his car and quad.

Despite all of these efforts and fun memories, the truth is, sharing hobbies is a far cry from truly getting to know someone.

That is probably why, as a child, I remember often being frustrated during some of my visits to my dad's house. As an example, Dad hated Velcro shoes and refused to buy them for me, leaving me with no choice but to learn how to tie my own laces. I was angry when he insisted that training wheels had no place beneath the steel frame of my bicycle, especially when my knees and shins would often beg to differ. And sometimes I really did not want to finish my plate of spaghetti before eating ice cream.

Dad insisted that we read every word before turning the page in a book, and he never let winter weather keep us inside. Even if my toes went numb.

When I became a teenager, his opinions and way of life did not change much. Dad hated cell phones (seriously—he still does not own one), didn't own a computer, and only once took me to my favorite drive-through for a cheeseburger and french fries. He always insisted that we go outside, spend time together, play games, and eat all of my stepmother's home-cooked meals. Together.

The audacity, I know.

This might all sound good now, but often my dad's lack of adaptation to the "real world" was infuriating to me. Looking back, I think it was infuriating because I didn't really know him then the way I know him today. Without really knowing him, it was hard to appreciate him.

As I got a little older, more experienced, and less selfish, I started to realize that all of these things I once labeled weird or outdated are what make my dad who he is. And who he is, as many know, is really special. That includes his marriage to my stepmother, Alison.

In my adult years, I have fondly described Dad as a simple man who does not need or want much to enjoy life. He and Alison have spent the last thirty-plus years enjoying nature, cooking over an open fire, and gardening in their front yard, and I have always loved the obvious joy it has brought them both. I guess that's why I should not have been so surprised about a recent conversation I shared with my dad.

He came to visit us in Missouri, and one evening over dinner, I asked him what the hardest thing he'd ever been through was. Although Dad typically avoids emotional conversations like the plague, I knew that based on the look on his face, he was ready to talk. And let me tell you, I was burning with curiosity about his answer.

Much to my relief, he was receptive to the question—which I knew was the first major hurdle. But before he gave me his answer, he paused, took a deep and drawn-out breath, and quickly blinked away the tears that filled his eyes. We were seated at a busy outdoor patio, but I swear to you that time stood still. What came next not only surprised and inspired me but also brought a lot of what I thought I knew about my dad into context.

I fully expected his answer to be the sudden death of his parents, his time spent serving in the army, his divorce from my mom and subsequent relationship with Alison, the challenge of co-parenting, or even one of the major accidents that either he, my brother, or I had had. But no. None of those moments are what immediately came to his mind.

Instead, he shared the details of the day Ryan drove out of the driveway for the first time. He described what it felt like to watch Ryan look in the rearview mirror, put the truck in reverse, and slowly inch away from where my dad stood. You could see both the light and the pain in his eyes as he described this event.

I'm sure that Ryan, as a newly licensed teen driver, couldn't wait to put his black Chevy S-10 truck into drive, but for my dad it was clearly a completely different and far more difficult experience. Naturally, I asked him what, above all else, made this so difficult for him. And naturally, he tiptoed around his answer and repeatedly told me he didn't know—until finally he admitted that the moment had made him feel like he was completely alone.

He quickly choked back more tears, took a sip of his beer, made a deflecting joke, and proceeded to defend his answer. He told me he assumed I'd been expecting something more dramatic or momentous. But little did he know, his answer provided greater insight than even I was expecting.

As it turns out, I was still getting to know my dad.

You see, like I said, my dad has always gravitated toward the simple. But not because he was outdated or resistant to change. It's because he embraces what others—like myself—can so easily take for granted as obvious or expected. During this same visit, Dad, my son, my husband, and I all went on a walk one morning. During this walk I found myself getting annoyed because Dad wanted to literally stop and smell all the roses I'd personally walked by hundreds of times without smelling. After all, I thought, if you've smelled one rose, you've smelled them all. I was anxious to keep walking, but Dad appeared to be both oblivious to my annoyance and lacking the same urgency I felt.

I frequently passed by the roses without stopping, but for my dad the roses in bloom were a chance for him to experience life a little more deeply. To breathe in and appreciate the simplicity of the day. Before I could make my objection known, he parked my son's stroller, lifted him out of it, and headed over to the pink rosebushes to breathe it all in. Standing back, Michael and I exchanged a half-hearted smile, shrugged our shoulders, and stood there as Dad took in the moment for all it was worth.

And suddenly, I understood—and the experience became full of meaning.

Now I can't walk past a rosebush without feeling a warmth in my heart. It reminds me of that moment where my dad taught my son—and reminded me—the power of a simple experience, like smelling a rose.

The older I've become, the more I've learned about my dad. And what I am learning makes me love him more and more every single day. I'm also discovering many qualities about him that I hope to emulate in my own life.

Dad once told me that the secret to a good life is to make every day last as long as possible. He also taught me, time and time again, that you have all you need right in front of you to be able to feel and experience the true meaning and joy of life. The obvious is only as simple as you allow it to be.

Thank you, Dad.

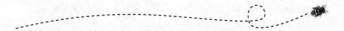

Dear Little Bee,

Your life will be filled to the brim with the big moments. You will have momentous occasions like birthdays, graduations, and holidays, and achievements that will be looked forward to and celebrated by many, including you, for the rest of your life.

But please do not wait for those moments to experience joy. Do not forget to cherish all the little, obvious, in-between moments too. I promise you, there is beauty and meaning in all of it.

As you go through life, I hope you can find ways to stop and smell the roses. And discover plenty of opportunities to tune out the "real world." And when you do, I pray you can take advantage of the seemingly obvious moments and fill them with both joy and meaning.

Like the way the sun feels on your face in the summer, or the way the leaves smell on a fresh fall morning. Even the feeling of sitting around a dinner table, eating a meal with those you love most.

I also hope you celebrate all of the things you maybe once thought you could not do, like ride a bike without training wheels or tie a shoe with real laces.

Your Pap often says that life is too short to go through it miserable, and he is right. I hope and pray you find happiness in all the ways to see, smell, feel, embrace, and celebrate life's simple moments. If you do, I know you will be filled with the simple joy that I love so much about your Pap.

A Verse for When You're Looking for Meaning

The LORD's acts of mercy are not exhausted, his compassion is not spent; they are renewed each morning—great is your faithfulness! (Lamentations 3:22–23 NABRE)

Questions for When You're Looking for Meaning

- What are two small things you could do today to make yourself happy?
- What is something simple or small that happened recently that you can celebrate?
- What is something simple that has brought your life meaning?

Dance that dance of simple joy.

PART TWO

YOUR STINGS

6

WHEN YOUR PLANS FOR LIFE AREN'T WORKING

God Has a Plan—Trust It

Most people can relate to the idea that we go through life with some sort of timeline for ourselves in mind. Somewhere along the way we dream up—or even vision-board out—an order of steps that must be adhered to. As an example, for me it looked like this: grow up, go to college, get a good job so you never worry about money, date so you can find someone to marry, have babies with that someone, live a life with that someone, and then, well, eventually die.

It's a to-do list that most of us feel like we need to check off well before we ever reach thirty (minus the dying part).

Dear reader, if you listen to nothing else I have to say, please listen to this:

There is no timeline.

I've mentioned that I grew up knowing I wanted more. In hindsight, I realize that was partly why I was so motivated in college to get good grades and land the best internships so I could ultimately secure the steadiest career. But part of that wanting more was also wanting a marriage that would last. My mom had been married and divorced three times, so it goes without saying I was adamant not to allow history to repeat itself. I did not want to endure all the heartache and struggle I watched her go through.

In no way do I view the desire for more as a bad thing, but for me, there became an unnecessary urgency to figure it all out. It led me down an inauthentic path that ended with hurt and required much-needed redirection.

So now that you know that about me, let's get into my story a bit deeper.

I met my now ex-husband in the spring of my sophomore year in college. I was twenty years old and very much in the mindset of wanting to find love. I was what they called an "old soul," so *of course* this meant that at this point in my life, I knew exactly what I wanted and who I wanted to spend my life with. (I hope you can sense my sarcasm here.)

On paper we were everything anyone could assume would last forever. We had fun together, enjoyed similar hobbies, and had the support of just about everyone around us. It was not uncommon for people to tell me just how lucky I was and warn me I'd better not screw this relationship up. And I understood why—he was a great guy, and I was lucky to have him.

Things were good and easy enough. But there was often a nagging voice in my head wondering if *this* was really *it*. And by *it*, I mean what true love was supposed to feel like. I wasn't aware that I was using my talent of shaping public perception not just to manipulate the opinions of those around me, but also my own. I genuinely believed a relationship could not get any better than the one I was in, because my boyfriend was such a great person. So I convinced myself that I must not be capable of feeling love the way in which I'd heard others describe it. I was afraid that this was as good as it could possibly get for me, and I didn't want to have the same fate as my mom. So, after five years of dating, my boyfriend and I got engaged, and after another year or so, we were married.

The wedding was almost perfect. I'd spent months going over every detail so that my wedding day would rival the best seen on the internet. There was no detail overlooked, no minute unaccounted for, and certainly no room for error. Once again, I would use my professional training to overly orchestrate a very personal occasion in my life.

Our wedding day was a typical beautiful summer day in Western Pennsylvania. The ceremony would take place less than a few miles from my dad and Alison's house, and I was surrounded by my closest girlfriends and family. The champagne was flowing and everyone was doting on me left and right. All was going completely as planned and then, all of a sudden, there was a notable energy shift and it became a not-according-to-plan series of events.

There was one person I wanted to be there more than anyone else that day—my grandmother. I know she wanted to be there too, because even though she was in her late eighties at the time and had been advised by doctors not to travel, she'd defiantly boarded a plane from Florida to Pennsylvania just days before the ceremony so she could be there for the occasion.

But apparently, God had a different plan. The morning of the wedding, my grandmother was found by the hotel staff almost completely unconscious in her room. Her perfectly manicured hands, with her infamous bright-yellow polished nails, were near lifeless as she was loaded into an ambulance and rushed to a nearby hospital. I received news of what had happened just hours before I was supposed to walk down the aisle.

In between dabs of a makeup sponge, tears fell from my eyes as reality sunk in. Not only would my grandmother miss the entire day, but there was also a very real possibility that she would not be with us here on this earth for much longer. Everyone around me did their best to put on a brave face, but I could feel the seriousness of the situation. It was bad. Really, really bad. The thought that my big day could be the cause of my grandmother's death was crippling, and it sent me spiraling.

It was at this moment that my aunt Missy gently pulled me aside, away from the group, looked me in the eyes, grabbed my shoulders, and said, "God has a plan." Aunt Missy has always been a source of support, love, and friendship in my life. We have always had a special bond, and I look up to her in many ways. She and my uncle Bernie have always been an inspiring example of marriage, God, and family values to me. But, unlike anyone else in my life, Aunt Missy has always had the unique ability to calm my heart and re-center me whenever life feels out of control. So, while I definitely appreciated her heartfelt reassurance in that moment, no part of me could understand what plan would involve this turn of events and the absence of my closest person on what was supposed to be the biggest day of my life.

The day, however, would not wait for me to understand. I dried my tears, held the pastor's hand as we prayed for my grandmother's health, and then linked arms with my dad to walk down the aisle. With every step, I could feel my grandmother's absence. I did my best to focus on the day, but there was little that could distract me from the seriousness of the situation.

The next day, I made my way to the hospital. My then-husband and I were supposed to be going on our honeymoon, but I refused to board the plane without seeing my grandmother first. I carried my wedding dress into the hospital because I thought she would want to see it, and I waited patiently for the doctor. Peering through the window into her room, I noticed how fragile she looked. She was asleep. She was dying.

The doctor greeted me and told me he thought it would be best if I said goodbye. Her situation was dire, and he was less than optimistic. I made my way into the room and held Grammy's hand. As I sat there, the only thing I could feel was the warmth of my tears on my own cheeks.

I didn't say goodbye; instead, I told her that I loved her and would see her when I got home. As it turned out, I was right.

A week later, my grandmother miraculously recovered, as she had a habit of doing. The celebrations were over and the next chapter of my life was beginning. The only problem was, as I returned to my new home state of Tennessee, the voice inside my head that had long been questioning my relationship never completely quieted. At the time, I didn't understand why. I felt like I should be happy and content, but I was not. In between traveling the world and having fun with my new husband, there was a noticeable void that refused to go away. A connection that struggled to be formed. I had a friendship with my husband, but I was feeling more and more certain that this was not the great love I wanted for my life.

And that is why deep down, when the dust settled, I knew I was struggling to be truly happy. But at the time, I didn't think it mattered. I wanted a successful marriage. And I was determined that I would not fail. What would people think if it didn't work out? This relationship would have to be good enough. And it wasn't as if I were *completely* miserable in the marriage. Plus, *tick-tock* went the timeline.

The year was 2020. We'd been married for less than two years before we decided to call it quits. It was one of the hardest yet most honest decisions I've ever made. Hard in all of the obvious ways, but easy in the sense that I knew I was not capable of loving this man the way in which he deserved. I also knew I could not live the rest of my life pretending that this love was my forever love, or always wondering if there could be more. And even though at this point I did not know if I wanted to be a mom, I knew that if I were to become one, the type of marriage I had was not one I wanted to model for my child.

I'd never felt worse in my entire life.

Most people think that getting a divorce only happens when something egregious happens, when one partner is the victim of a selfish act. None of that was true in my case. Nothing bad had happened, and my ex-husband was far from a bad person. In fact, if anyone could be blamed for the demise of our marriage, it was me.

Because for me, "good enough" was not good enough. I wanted a friendship *and* a great love. I didn't want to sacrifice one for the other.

The unavoidable next step was to tell people what was happening. Some calls were easier to make than others. But there was one I dreaded more than the others: the call to Uncle Bernie and Aunt Missy. Not because I thought they would be mad at me, but because I was afraid they would be disappointed in me. I was so afraid I'd let them down. I could handle most of the people who did not agree with my decision, but this felt different.

I remember pulling off to the side of the road that day to make the call. My heart was beating so fast, and I felt sick to my stomach with every ring of the phone. When Aunt Missy finally picked up, I'm sure I caught her by surprise when, sobbing, I told her what was going on.

She listened, she comforted, and she reminded me that *God has a plan.*

As you can imagine, this part of my life gave me plenty to think about. Leading up to, during, and after the divorce were some of the darkest and loneliest moments I've ever felt. I was far from proud of myself. Heck, I even started to question who "myself" really was. I had done something I swore I would never do. *Divorce.* I was hurting. I had caused hurting.

Some of my family and friends were supportive; some were not. As a result, I spent more time inside my own head than anywhere else. Which was also fitting for the year. Because 2020 and the notorious global pandemic forced almost all of us into isolation.

I went on a lot of walks during that time. Like, *a lot* of walks. Some with a friend, but most alone.

I spent miles and miles going over things in my head. I asked myself the obvious questions: How did I get here? Why did I ever say yes if I hadn't been completely sure? Was I actually sure now? Was I making the biggest mistake of my life?

As my feet hit the pavement, much to my surprise, I eventually felt twinges of clarity emerging and a subsequent peace that had long been absent. It was during these walks that I started to realize that in the relentless pursuit of my self-authored timeline and storyline, I never once slowed down long enough to ask myself the hard questions about the relationship and listen to my own honest answers.

The hard truth was that once again, I found myself in a place of wanting more. More from my life and more from my marriage. I did not just want a marriage that would last. I wanted a marriage that would fulfill. And unfortunately, the person I had committed to was not the answer. I had placed a safe bet from a place of comfort and fear, and I had lost that bet.

I recognized that the "how I got here" part was incredibly reflective of just how unwilling I was to let life happen. It wasn't God's plan; it was my own plan. And I firmly believed I knew best.

As time went on, during these walks I also started to recognize and appreciate the growth in myself. Who I had been ten years ago was not who I was today, and I began to realize just how good of a thing that was. Despite the missteps and mistakes, I began to feel proud of my evolution. Plus, I think life is far too short to only know one version of yourself.

For instance, a big part of my evolution was wanting to lean into my faith more. I was raised Catholic and believed in God, but I'd truthfully never taken the time to build a relationship with Him. There is a difference. To be intentional about having a relationship with God required a prioritization that had long been absent in my life. I guess if I am being honest, it was never really there to begin with.

Lucky for us, God is always waiting to pull us back from the darkness. In fact, a dear friend has often reminded me that God does His best work there. If you think about it, the darker a room is, the brighter a light will shine. Beyond that, one of my biggest beliefs is that God will get you through your darkest times so you can then turn around and be the light for the person behind you.

After going through my divorce, I had a handful of conversations with friends, and even strangers, who had unfortunately found themselves in a similar situation to the one I'd just been through. Some were recently married and now were in the process of going through a divorce, some were ready to call off an engagement, and others were still trying to find their person and were worried that time was running out. Although we all had somewhat different circumstances, there was a commonality regarding the presence of a self-imposed timeline and the absence of faith in the plan created for us. Rarely did I find someone in this situation who was simply willing to let life happen. In our own different ways, we were all in a rush to figure out answers that were never really ours to begin with.

Maybe that is because letting life happen—or more importantly, learning to trust in God's plan—can be incredibly difficult. Especially when we are worried or anxious. Especially when we think we are running out of time.

In fact, as I started writing this chapter, my three-month-old son was quietly napping next to me. Those first few months with a newborn had been absolutely blissful, but also freaking exhausting. And it didn't help when my husband and I thought there was a chance we could be pregnant again.

Do not get me wrong—welcoming another baby into this world would be nothing short of a blessing, but it was not exactly something we had planned for that soon. Or ever.

My point is this. After having my complete melt-down, which I would like to partly blame on hormones and lack of sleep, I started to realize how hypocritical, yet human, my immediate reaction was. Here I was typing away at my great philosophy of life and how it's God's plan, not our own—and in one moment of "not according to my own plan," I was back to relying on my own version versus trusting His. It was a quick and harsh reminder that often, the best thing we can do in uncertain moments is pray. When we pray, we ask for God's direction and strength, and that we will accept whatever He has in store for us.

That day, as my emotions leveled back out and clarity once again emerged through prayer, I remembered my aunt Missy's advice: *God has a plan.* Whatever His plan is for you, He will also equip you to handle it. Ultimately, my husband and I did not conceive another child, but never underestimate the power of a learning moment.

I really saw the beauty of God's perfect timing when I received an unexpected gift from my aunt Missy. As I mentioned before, my grandmother tragically passed away before I married Michael. I hated the fact that she never got to meet him. I also worried what she would have thought about my divorce and how she would have felt about the love Michael and I shared.

And then one day, I did not have to wonder any-more. Aunt Missy handed me a letter that had been written by my grandmother in her beautiful cursive handwriting. I had never seen it before, and I was not sure when exactly it had been written. But at that moment, it felt like the kindest gift my aunt could have given me. She'd given me one more chance to hear my grandmother.

> *Courtney darling, you are not my birth child. But to me, you are not just my granddaughter. There are so many memories of you when you were my baby. When you succeed, I feel joy. When you are unhappy, I cry. Someday God will send you a very special person who will love you and make you happy. I may not be here to see it, but know I am always with you. I do love you so much.*

Thank you, Aunt Missy.

Dear Little Bee,

Life is for living, not for rushing or overplanning.

Having goals and aspirations for your life is a lot different than having a plan. Especially if that plan is absent of faith. Do not worry about, or rush to, the answers you are seeking in life. Trust that they will come, and try to be patient. Use your energy to focus on your relationship with God and trust in His plans for you above your own.

I know that trusting God's plan will be a lot easier for you when things are going well, but even when things are hard or feel like they're veering off course, remember, He is still in control, and He does work all things together for good.

I once read that God doesn't ask you to figure it out—He asks you to trust that He already has. You will learn that it takes a lot of discipline to give up your desire to control the uncontrollable. But it is worth it. Because sometimes when things do not go as we planned them to, they actually turn out better than we could have imagined.

Your journey is uniquely yours, and you are equipped to handle it. Do not waste time worrying about what other people think. I promise that those who love you will support you.

You will find your forever person, so don't force it or rush it. If you are wondering if there is more, there probably is. "Good enough" never has to be good enough for you. Keep evolving and do not settle.

And do not forget, sometimes the perfect plan is better off perfectly failing.

Verses for When Your Plans for Life Aren't Working

"For I know the plans I have for you," declares the LORD, "plans to prosper and not to harm you, plans to give you hope and a future." (Jeremiah 29:11 NIV)

Even though you meant harm to me, God meant it for good. (Genesis 50:20 NABRE)

Questions for When Your Plans for Life Aren't Working

- When is a time in your life where things turned out better than you had planned?
- How do you respond to life not going according to your plan?
- How would you feel if instead of trying to control things yourself, you let go and trusted God?

Inspiration for When Your Plans for Life Aren't Working

"What's not meant for you will miss you. Maybe it's all working out for you beautifully, in ways you can't put into words, in perspectives that only become visible in retrospect. So, don't force it all to happen the way you think it should. Be open to it unfolding better than expected." —Jamie Varon (adapted from an Instagram post)

Dance that dance of faith and patience.

7

WHEN YOU ARE STUCK IN YOUR PAST

Keep Moving Forward

I moved to Tennessee from Detroit for a new job opportunity during the spring of 2018. It would be the second time I had relocated with my company since I was hired by them right out of college, and my country-music-loving soul could not have been more excited. Although this would be the furthest I had ever lived from home, something inside me knew this was the right next step for me. I was in my midtwenties at the time and had a thirst for new adventure that could rarely be fully quenched. Plus, I'd grown up on the back of a horse, hated the cold, and knew just about every word to every country song that played on the radio, so clearly, it was time to take my life south.

Prior to officially relocating to Tennessee, I had the chance to visit the area, meet my new team, and find a place to live. Aside from those essentials, one of the first things I wanted to do was find a local gym to join. I had found this to be an easy way to meet people, and exercise has always been important to me.

After a quick internet search, I found myself at the entrance of a local CrossFit gym. Walking into a new gym is never comfortable and always a little awkward. It is also worth noting that I, too, am always a little awkward. Luckily for me, Southern hospitality extended into the CrossFit world, and it was not long before I'd made several new friends, many of whom I am still close with today.

It's always fascinating to look back on your life and think about the chain of events that led one moment to the next. This was one of those moments for me. Had I never been offered the job in Tennessee, I never would have walked into this gym, and if I hadn't walked into this gym, I never would have met some of the most amazing friends I've ever had. And I certainly never would have met Gina, who my son lovingly refers to as "Aunt Gina." And if I'd never met Gina, I don't know how I would have ever survived my divorce and subsequently grown stronger in my faith. I also probably wouldn't have learned how to make delicious fettuccine alfredo, discovered the many uses of coconut oil, or been given such good guidance on how to breastfeed my baby. Seriously, our friendship knows no boundaries. Needless to say, life without Gina is not something I ever want to sign up for.

At the time we met, Gina was already a mother of four and was expecting her fifth child, Gia, any day. She and her husband, Bernard, are pillars of their community and adored by many. When we first met, on paper Gina and I were about as different as they come—but as time went on and we started doing more things together, my admiration for her grew.

She loved, believed, and gave fearlessly. She made people feel at ease and comforted them. She constantly went out of her way to make things better for others and never hesitated to open her home to someone in need. The more I learned about Gina, the more I wanted her in my life forever. Which is why I knew she was the one person I had to be honest with.

When I first met Gina, I was still married to my ex-husband. We had moved to Tennessee together after our wedding, and it was only a year later when things started to decline. After I made the decision to file for divorce, Gina was one of the first people I chose to tell. I remember being incredibly nervous about how she would react. Here she was, a beautiful mother of five children, with a solid marriage and a faith stronger than an oak tree. And she would be the first to tell you that she believes in marriage and that divorce was not necessarily something she supported. For all these reasons and more, I was anxious about talking to her.

I did not want to lose Gina. I couldn't. Not now. I knew that once I shared my story with her, it would be a deciding point in our friendship. We would either continue down the path we had started on, or it would be time to go our separate ways.

I was surprised but relieved by her reaction. As I found the courage to share, she listened intently and only offered her prayers and support in return. I did not feel judged; I felt safe. I felt loved. I felt lightened. I had always admired Gina's faith and knew that was something I wanted to learn more about and have more of in my life. It was one of her many qualities I wanted to emulate. One evening, as I was sitting and chatting with her in her home after attending one of her children's soccer games, she handed me a daily devotional that had been given to her a few years prior. Titled *Jesus Calling*, it was a red leather-bound book, and each day had a short message with accompanying verses. She told me that a friend had given her this book when she was going through a difficult time, and that maybe it would serve me in the same way it had helped her. I am sure that by this point in our relationship, I'd mentioned wanting to explore faith more, and this felt like a safe place to start. Deep down, I think she knew that too.

For the next several days, *Jesus Calling* was the first thing I read every morning. I found myself excited just to wake up and see what the message of the day would be. I was in awe. I was excited. I was hopeful. I was learning.

From that moment on, Gina began to regularly speak truth into my life. She shared God's Word, reminding me of whose I really was—and often reminding me that His plan for me was ultimately still unfolding. Gina told me that like a flower, I could bloom again. She never once made me feel like I was an inconvenience, or like she was tired of listening to my fears and concerns. I turned to her for advice and reassurance in my high moments, in my low moments, and in all my moments in between. Right before my eyes, God gave me a sister.

I will never forget the day I was working from home and had my favorite broadcast news station on in the background. It was one of those days where the light coming in through my apartment windows mirrored the light I felt in my heart. It had taken a long time, but I finally felt good again. I was still very vulnerable and highly sensitive to anything I perceived as a sign indicating either a right or wrong direction in my life. So you can imagine my surprise when the news segment of the day was about divorced couples who decided to give it another try and recommit after so many years of separation. Those who know me would not be surprised by how I reacted—I broke out in a cold sweat, with my infamous sweaty palms and a pit in my stomach. I wondered if this was God's way of telling me, "Wrong way!"

To deal with the situation, I did what I do best. I picked up my phone and messaged Gina. And her response?

"The devil knows where, when, and how to get you. Forward."

Part of me was stunned by her brevity. But the words-of-affirmation, needy side of me wanted more. However, rather than push it, I sat with her message. There was a confidence in her succinctness, and it caught my attention. By this point, I had spent months trying to understand how God works—and not much time at all trying to understand that in direct opposition, we have the enemy. At this moment, my guard was down and the enemy took his chance. He was creative, but with Gina's help, I changed the channel. I turned to faith.

My initial reaction to the news segment that day was thinking it was the universe telling me I'd made a huge mistake, even though I had no desire to get back together with my ex. Gina's response that day may not have been the kind of answer I was hoping for, but it turns out it was even better. It inspired me to learn more. It set me up for a future of forwards.

Since then, I have come to believe that if your thoughts are full of love, hope, forgiveness, and light, you should trust that they are from God. However, if your thoughts are full of self-doubt, guilt, shame, and anxiety, they probably aren't from Him. Because of Gina, I now believe that God is less interested in our past and much more interested in our future. In Isaiah 43:18–19, He tells us, "Forget the former things; do not dwell on the past. See, I am doing a new thing! Now it springs up; do you not perceive it? I am making a way in the wilderness and streams in the wasteland" (NIV).

I have also learned that we should never underestimate the creativity of the enemy to bring us down.

On this seemingly ordinary day while I was sitting at my kitchen counter, despite the best attempts from the enemy to distract me, I was reminded by my sister-friend Gina that God wants us to move *forward*.

It's so easy to get caught up in what cannot be undone that we lose sight of what can be done. It is easy to let our minds wander and replay all of our what-ifs or should-have moments. But what if instead, we channeled that same energy to decide how we were going to go forward? What if instead of dwelling on the past, we picked up the pieces of what we learned and grew from them? Whether we like it or not, life is only moving in one direction, so isn't it time we allowed our minds to do the same?

Several years later, my dad and I were talking about the experience of learning to ride a bike for the first time. He mentioned the advice he'd shared with both my brother and me, as well as with many neighborhood kids who have since received his bicycle-riding instruction.

"It's simple. The direction you look is the direction you will go," he explained. "If you look down, you will fall down."

So maybe it's about not looking back either. If you focus on the past, you will continue to live in the past. My divorce is not something I can ever imagine being proud of, but I have promised myself to take what I have learned from that experience to be a better person. To move forward. But it is not always easy. In fact, even as I was writing this book, I was truly the happiest I'd ever been. However, if I'm being completely transparent, the truth is that if I let my mind wander too far, I catch myself going back to the dark places, to the pain of shame and fear.

Sometimes those thoughts would creep in late at night as I was trying to fall asleep, and sometimes they crept in as I sat happily watching my son and husband play together. Whenever I had them, I quietly whispered "forward" to myself, and then I thanked God for the chance to do better and for the friendships—like my friendship with Gina—that made it possible.

I'm not sure we can always control where our minds wander, but I will always do my best to choose *forward*.

Thank you, Gina.

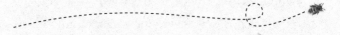

Dear Little Bee,

By now you know your aunt Gina and the love she brings to our lives. And by now, you know a little bit more about why this relationship is so special to me and to our family.

As you go through life, it is inevitable that you will make mistakes. First and foremost, I want you to know that your dad and I will always have your back. We will always love you.

I also want you to remember that you can move forward from anything. In fact, you have to. Life is for forward motion.

It is important that you know that the devil knows where, when, and how to get to you. When negative thoughts pop into your head, I want you to change the channel. Instead, focus on God's Word and promise for your life. Of course, none of this is easy. But I promise, it is doable.

Lastly, surround yourself with people who remind you of and show you God's love. I want you to find the kind of friends who offer you a hand when you've lost your way and the kind of friends who turn into family—friends who you have no idea how you ever lived without.

Forward, Little Bee. Always, forward.

Verses for When You Are Stuck in Your Past

And we know that all things work together for good to them that love God, to them who are the called according to his purpose. (Romans 8:28 KJV)

Forgetting what is behind and straining toward what is ahead, I press on toward the goal to win the prize for which God has called me heavenward in Jesus Christ. (Philippians 3:13–14 NIV)

Questions for When You Are Stuck in Your Past

- What can you do about the thing that has already been done?
- Is what you are thinking a feeling? Or a fact? How are these thoughts making you feel?
- Do you have friends in your life who love Jesus and demonstrate His love?
- How can you show someone else the love of Jesus?

Inspiration for When You Are Stuck in Your Past

"It isn't failure that holds you back. It's the emotional baggage you carry afterward. Self-doubt, regret, disappointment, and embarrassment are instruction manuals for learning. The goal isn't to dwell on what went wrong yesterday. It's to discover what you can do today." —Adam Grant (adapted from an Instagram post)

Dance your dance in forward motion.

8

WHEN YOU LACK CONFIDENCE ABOUT YOUR CHOICES

You Don't Need Their Validation

I met Lex during my sophomore year of college. I had arrived on campus later than everyone else that year due to my summer internship, and my late arrival happened to give my lifelong best friend, Katie, a chance to meet other people in my absence. It was a typical gray and rainy day in Western Pennsylvania when Katie and I hopped onto the campus shuttle bus and she was a little too excited to introduce me to her new friend and roommate, Lex. While I did my very best to project confidence, there was absolutely no confidence present as I was introduced to this beautiful, funny, outgoing woman who was obviously moving in on my territory of being Katie's best friend.

"I don't like her," I quickly told Katie after we arrived at school.

I now know that was my ego speaking. Because fast-forward more than a decade later, and that girl I didn't like has become easily one of my closest friends. In fact, I can confidently tell you that my friendship with Lex continues to enrich my life daily.

There is a lot to love about Lex and our friendship. For starters, the time we invest in each other is intentional. That is one of the many blessings of having long-distance friendships. And a friendship with Lex *is* a true blessing, because she is easily one of the most genuine and grounded people I know. Since day one, what I have always admired most about her is how methodically she moves through life. Whether it is her food choices, relationships, or even her career path, every step she takes is diligent and well thought out. She is not afraid to take her time with things and has never been hesitant to start over.

Clearly, these are qualities I admire and could probably stand to adopt a bit more myself. Lex has always had an undeniable and intentional amount of patience. I love that about her. I also love that our friendship is one that allows us to sometimes see things that the other person can't and gives us a safe place to call them out on it. For example, when one of us finds herself in a desperate, fruitless, downward spiral, endlessly seeking external validation.

The truth is, I was really worried about what people would think about my divorce and subsequent decision to begin a relationship with Michael so quickly. Specifically, I was worried about what they would think about our age difference. I wondered, and in some ways obsessed over, what people may or may not have been saying, because it *was* different. I wasn't sure if people would understand, and I didn't know how I would explain my feelings if they did not.

To make matters more difficult, neither my dad nor my brother had been totally on board with my decision to end my previous marriage. I will admit, it was for understandable reasons. They were close with my ex, and I am sure in a lot of ways, they saw that marriage as the perfect situation and addition to our family. My decision to get a divorce blindsided many people, but none quite as much as my dad and Ryan.

And then it came time for me to tell them about dating Michael, a man almost nineteen years older than me and a close colleague of mine. And by close, I mean that at one point, just prior to us dating, I indirectly reported to him.

When I think back to the day when I told Dad and Ryan about Michael, no expression rings quite as true as "that went over like a lead balloon." Their reactions were tough to take, but my dad's was definitely the strongest, and his disapproval weighed on me heavily. I wanted his support, and it was clear I didn't have it. For months, Dad and I argued, ignored, and argued some more about my new reality. There were dead silences, abruptly ended phone calls, and a clear agitation any time the topic of "Michael" was mentioned. The strain on our relationship was unlike anything we'd ever experienced before.

Dad and I were at complete odds, neither of us wanting to back down. He was coming from a place of concern, as he was my father and was worried about what this age difference meant for my future and my career. And I was hell-bent on him understanding that what I was feeling was bigger than any of his concerns. I was angry that he didn't understand, because I'd known pretty quickly that Michael was the love of my life. Falling in love with Michael ignited parts of my soul that I didn't think even existed.

Yet the reality was that my dad's skepticism and lack of support made it almost impossible not to question my own feelings and decisions. I couldn't recall a time when I'd ever made a major life decision without first having Dad's approval. This was likely the first time it had happened. And it was a big one. I am sure that to some, this may not seem out of the ordinary. But for me, it was.

Growing up, I was very used to being the person who did things for the "popular vote." Like many people, I often found myself making decisions because I knew other people would approve of them or because they would "look good" to the outside world. I specifically always wanted the approval of both my dad and my brother. I always admired them, and I still do. When I was younger, it was not uncommon for me to measure my success based on their reactions and happiness. This habit started when I was a teenager and followed me well into my twenties.

It wasn't just trying to do what everyone else did that was the problem—it was trying to do what everyone else would *approve of.*

So here I was, decades later, still very much going about my life in the same way. Extremely focused on the opinions of others and holding my breath for my dad and brother to say "good job."

I tried to play it cool. I tried to put on a brave face that said, "I am not concerned with the opinions of others," and while I may have fooled some, I definitely was not fooling myself. I was really struggling.

At the time, there were very few people in my life with whom I felt comfortable enough to be completely honest and vulnerable. Lex was one of them. There were plenty of times when I would call and talk to her about my worries and insecurities, and I'm sure that a lot of my grievances were redundant, but she always listened intently like it was the first time she was hearing them.

It was during one of these conversations when Lex stopped me, challenged me, and gave me a safe place to see things differently.

And what I realized that day was exhilarating, empowering, and downright terrifying: the opinions of those we love are important, but so is finding the place where we can take those opinions in and still make confident choices for ourselves, through the filter of our own knowledge and heart. I saw the power behind the ability to tune out what other people may or may not think, and tune in to what I felt instead.

As soon as I accepted this, I realized that I owed no one an explanation. And that felt really good. Self-validation is a thing.

Several months and multiple heated conversations later, my dad finally saw it—the love I had been trying so hard to explain. And not only did he see it, but he accepted and embraced it with an open heart. I stood in my truth, validated my own damn self, and finally we were there. I had both the greatest love of my life *and* the acceptance of my dad. It wasn't easy, but at the risk of sounding overly cliché, it was worth it. What sounds so simple was perhaps one of the most complex journeys and realizations I have ever had.

Years later, I was walking past my bathroom mirror one morning when a very ordinary object caught my attention. In a cheap black frame, just next to my toothbrush holder, sat a handwritten note on a half-torn sheet of paper that read: *The mirror is for when you get up in the morning. As long as you're happy with what you see, we're all good!!!* I had probably walked past this note a hundred times. But on this day, it felt different. My dad had written this note, and he'd given it to me on the day I graduated from college. These were the words of encouragement he'd shared with me any time I would call him, stressed out about classes or assignments, or when I worried that whatever I was doing wouldn't make him proud.

As I sat there staring at this note over a decade later, rereading his simple yet powerful words, I couldn't help but chuckle. Dad had been teaching me how to validate myself all along.

Oh, the irony.

But there is a reason why I keep that note by my mirror, even today. It is my constant reminder that sometimes all we can do is try our best and trust that our best is good enough. Other people will always have opinions, but being able to look at yourself, know that your intentions are pure, and feel good about whatever it is you are doing, is sometimes the only reassurance you need. Or, quite frankly, the only reassurance you will get.

That reminder and reassurance continued to serve a purpose in the months that followed. My dad and brother may have been tough critics, but they were not the only ones. Truthfully, my relationship with Michael had always felt like a constant uphill battle. Even during our happiest moments, it always felt like there was someone trying to knock us down. Someone who would inevitably not find joy in our happiness.

When we got engaged, I worried about how people would react.

When we got pregnant, I found myself holding my breath when we shared the news.

When we got married, there were empty seats at the wedding.

Even though I knew it was all worth it, and that it was somewhat understandable, it didn't make it any less exhausting.

Before I knew it, I was starting to get resentful and envious of other people I knew and how effortlessly they appeared to live their lives. Maybe more traditional relationships were the answer, because it didn't seem like anyone else had to endure what Michael and I were going through. I was becoming bitter and starting to feel defeated.

What I didn't initially realize was that it wasn't other people causing the problem. It was my own mindset that was the dark cloud I couldn't get out from under. And no, I didn't come to that realization alone. At the peak of these emotions, I knew I needed someone who loved me and who could offer a different perspective than what I was capable of seeing on my own. So once again, I called Lex. After listening to what I am sure was at least a thirty-minute rant about how everyone else's life was obviously much easier than mine, she paused and then without hesitation said, "Well, Courtney, we all have shit."

I busted out laughing. I wanted pity, but as it turns out, I needed reality. Those were the exact words I needed to hear, and I knew she was right. I had been so caught up with feeling sorry for myself, and only focusing on my own experiences, that I'd wrongfully sold myself the storyline that I was the only one who had any hardship to endure. Of course, that wasn't true. Life is uniquely hard, for all of us. Just because people weren't talking about it didn't mean it wasn't happening.

I guess sometimes the lessons we need to learn, or be reminded of, are the obvious ones.

When I was willing to set my self-pity aside, I felt lighter and more at peace than I'd felt in months. The critics were still there, but my mindset had changed.

When I accepted that yes, I had difficulties just like everyone else on this earth, I also accepted that I had the power to decide the meaning I assigned to those difficulties, as well as where I would focus my attention.

That acceptance and control over my internal narrative reminded me that seasons of difficulty and waiting often have an unparalleled opportunity to grow us.

Because just like Lex said, *we all have shit*. Shit that feels unbearable, isolating, and downright unfair at times. But don't forget that shit can be a real teacher too. The way I see it is, you can either *go* or *grow* through life. I think there is a real opportunity to normalize using our shit as a fertilizer for better. And sometimes, better is just on the other side of the courage to validate yourself.

Thank you, Lex.

Dear Little Bee,

The never-ending need to be validated, or the tendency to compare, is one of the most crippling and isolating feelings you can experience in this lifetime. It is undoubtedly a dangerous trap to fall into.

So, I hope that instead, you choose to pray first, and look inward next. Find your truth and stand in it. Do the right thing, just because it's the right thing to do. Not because someone may or may not celebrate it.

The opinions of others are often none of your business, and definitely nothing you can control. The sooner you accept that, the better.

Remember that sometimes you may not be able to explain it, and often you don't need to. Look in the mirror. As long as you're happy with what you see, we're all good!

The somewhat obvious and unfortunate truth is that life is really hard for all of us. So, as you deal with your own inevitable difficulties and critics, accept that you can't always change your situation, but you can always change the meaning you assign it. If you need help, tell your mom. We may not always agree, but your dad and I will always love you.

And lastly, if I can give you any piece of advice, it would be to find friendships that challenge you to think differently without making you think any less of yourself.

Verses for When You Lack Confidence About Your Choices

Fear of man will prove to be a snare, but whoever trusts in the LORD is kept safe. (Proverbs 29:25 NIV)

On the contrary, we speak as those approved by God to be entrusted with the gospel. We are not trying to please people but God, who tests our hearts. (1 Thessalonians 2:4 NIV)

Questions for When You Lack Confidence About Your Choices

- Is what you are doing bringing you true happiness and joy? Or are you doing it to get the approval of others?
- Why are you really so concerned with what other people think? Do their thoughts actually impact your life?

- Are you doing your best in this situation? If yes, what things outside of your control can you let go of?
- Is your focus on God and on being honest with yourself? Or is your focus on the opinions of others?

Be confident in your own steps.

9

WHEN EVERYTHING FEELS IMPOSSIBLE

Iron Sharpens Iron

After a few years as a communications manager, I decided it was time for a change and chose to pursue an opportunity within the human resources and labor relations department at my company. For some, this might not seem like a significant move, but for me it certainly was. In the early stages of my career, I was someone who frequently sought out the path of least resistance, or maybe more accurately, the path of least risk. So, the idea of leaving what I knew and what I was good at for something new and challenging was simply terrifying.

From the moment I submitted my application, I instantly felt out of my league. But at the same time, I could not ignore how exciting the idea of pushing myself out of my comfort zone felt. I felt empowered by the fact that, for the first time in my career, I was truly embracing the unknown.

For weeks I studied every piece of literature about the job I could get my hands on. I would be attempting a totally new role that neither my experience nor my education had formally prepared me for. On the day of my interview, I met with three different directors, all of whom were seemingly skeptical of my capabilities. All except one, that is—the facility's director, Dan. As I looked across the table and answered the interviewers' questions, somehow I knew that Dan believed in me. Why he did, I will never know, but his confidence became my confidence.

Several days later, Dan greeted me at my desk and handed me an envelope with a handwritten note congratulating me on my new position. I'd done it. I'd gotten the job.

The team I joined was composed of several experienced human resources and labor relations professionals, none of whom seemed to be particularly enthused about me joining the team. And I can't say I blamed them. We were in the middle of a global pandemic, facing notorious supply chain shortages and implementing a new operating system. To say it was total chaos would be a complete understatement. The last thing they needed was a rookie like me joining the team.

Although understandable, the team's lack of enthusiasm only heightened and perpetuated my insecurities.

Thankfully, in a sea of doubters, Dan believed in me. And not only did he believe in me, but he invested in me, which made me want to work that much harder.

So I did.

I came in early and stayed late. I did the tasks that no one else on the team wanted to do, or had the time to do. I asked a lot of questions and listened as much as I could. I didn't try to be the best in the room; I tried to be the hardest-working and the most eager to learn. I tried to remember everything my mentors had taught me and, most importantly, I tried to be myself. The bottom line was that I wanted to prove to Dan, myself, and everyone else that I could do this job and do it well.

My team was directly responsible for all of the people in our organization, in addition to enforcing contractual obligations and labor laws. As a result, tensions were usually high and the problems we dealt with were always real. Problems like grown adults getting into fights in the parking lot, workers not getting paid correctly, and even employees pooping in garbage cans.

Yes, seriously.

Despite my best efforts, my lack of experience and the environment made the job extremely difficult. And by difficult, I mean that some days it felt like literal hell on earth. It became very clear to me early on that I was far from the land of corporate politeness and polish I'd once known. I consistently felt like I could not get anything right or even accomplish anything on my own. I still needed a lot of help and instruction, and that dependence chipped away at the little confidence I'd spent the past few years building. In fact, I can recall days where I would just drop my head in my hands and cry with frustration and exhaustion.

There were plenty of times when I wondered if I'd made a huge mistake taking on a new role. After all, my job in communications came so much more naturally to me. And there definitely was no poop. As the months went by, and I struggled to find my place on the team, my personal life was nothing short of a mess. I had separated from my ex-husband and subsequently had started dating Michael. In addition to the turmoil our relationship had caused in our own families, Michael and I were navigating what felt like a lot of criticism at work.

Because we worked together, Michael and I had done our best to keep our relationship private in the beginning. But our workplace seemed like the equivalent of a high school for middle-aged adults. Privacy did not exist, and rumors started to fly. Accusations and assumptions were a dime a dozen. It's not that I didn't expect it, but I'd been so caught up in trying to manage my new role that I wasn't prepared for it the way I should have been. In fact, I still remember the day when one of my favorite coworkers pulled me into a conference room and warned me that people were starting to talk about me and my relationship. As much as I'd tried to prepare for this inevitable moment and put on a brave

face, it didn't stop the pit in my stomach from forming or the waves of nausea from washing over me as he
shared the specifics of the rumors.

And as he talked, I instantly wanted to run out of
the room and correct people's storylines. Most of them
had it all wrong. Regardless, I wasn't used to knowingly
being the topic of conversation, and in no way did it
feel good. The feeling of desperation was strongest. I
was desperate for everyone else to know and believe my
version of the story, not theirs. I did my best to push
these feelings aside and not focus on the opinions of
others, but my insecurities were pouring out of me with
every drop of cold sweat. Unfortunately, this cycle of
rumors and insecurities would play on repeat for the
next several months. That time was incredibly difficult,
yet when I think back on this particular season of my
life, that is not what stands out to me now.

Instead, what I recall—and what I am so grateful
for—are the dozens of people I had standing in my corner. While there were plenty of people trying to bring
me down, I also had an army of people holding me up.
And, to no surprise, one of those people in my army was
the man on the other side of the proverbial table, Dan.

In addition to the investment he made in me profes-
sionally, he made an equal investment in me personally
and spiritually. The time Dan spent teaching me about
my new role soon evolved into deep discussions about
family and faith. He shared with me stories about his life,

including lessons he'd learned from his father. Through his stories, we grew closer and closer. Not only was I learning more about Dan, but I was learning more about the type of person I wanted to be. His presence felt like a light in my darkness.

One afternoon, on a particularly difficult day, I shared with Dan just how worn-out and discouraged I was feeling. Both about my new role and my new relationship. My tears could not be stopped. I had hit my breaking point. Everything felt ridiculously hard. I was frustrated, sad, and defeated. I was insecure. I didn't know what giving up would look like, but I felt like I was close.

Dan listened intently like he always did, and after I finished speaking, he calmly leaned across the table and asked me if I knew how to make a sword. Puzzled, I responded, "Absolutely not." With a smirk on his face, he then made a hammering gesture with his fists and told me, "You put the metal in a fire—hold it there until the metal becomes blazing hot, and then you beat the snot out of it. Over and over and over again."

The look on my face must have given away my confusion, because that is when Dan proceeded to share the encouragement his dad once shared with him, a reference to Proverbs 27:17 that, in part, states, "Iron sharpens iron."

Dan's father, Brigadier General Robinson Risner, was one of our nation's most decorated pilots in the

Korean and Vietnam wars. He spent over seven years as a prisoner of war in the infamous Vietnamese Hanoi Hilton prison. And for three of those years, he was kept in total darkness and solitary confinement. Dan spoke highly of his father's bravery and had shared many stories of his resilience. From these stories, I knew that if anyone might know what it felt like to be on the brink of giving up, it most definitely would be General Risner.

Although my experience was worlds apart from General Risner's, his words and tenacity inspired me. If he could endure something as terrible as what Dan described, then surely I could make my way through this, or any, season of difficulty.

I could be a sword.

From that moment on, I did my best to imagine every frustration, every hardship, every nasty rumor strengthening me. In moments of weakness, I would close my eyes and picture metal in a flame, or iron being beaten against iron. Admittedly, it wasn't an easy habit to form, but eventually, those days became a little more manageable.

My sword was starting to take shape.

With time and a lot of support, I became better at my job and more knowledgeable about the field. As a result, I was gaining confidence and respect. Thankfully, the rumors started to subside and my relationship became old news. Before I knew it, I wasn't just getting through it; I was emerging from it with a renewed perspective and strength.

This time of my life was undoubtedly another challenging chapter. Nothing about it felt easy. But looking back, I would not have had it any other way. I proved to myself that I could learn something new and accomplish hard things. I learned to focus less on the opinions of others and more on living my life authentically. Through hardship, I learned more about myself and, more importantly, about my faith. What a blessing it had all become.

To this day, I try to remember that experience and those lessons during moments or seasons of difficulty. And, to the best of my ability, instead of letting the weight of a situation crush me, I use it to sharpen me. I picture Dan at the other end of the table, smiling as he makes a hammering gesture with his fist.

Thank you, Dan.

Dear Little Bee,

Even though I will do my best to protect you, unfortunately, you will learn that life can be really hard. Sometimes we choose our hard; other times it is chosen for us.

Regardless, when you find yourself in the fire of life, I hope you can visualize your sword getting stronger.

Don't fall into the trap of thinking that the easiest path is the right one; often, there are way more rewarding options out there. It might just mean you have to fight your way through it for a while. Don't be afraid to try something challenging or to weather a storm for someone you love. It's worth it.

Similarly, accept that other people will always have their own versions of a story and, like their opinions, it isn't your responsibility to control them. In fact, when you relinquish the need to try to control something so uncontrollable, you give more room for what truly matters in your life.

Wherever you are, and wherever you choose to go, I pray that you will proceed with confidence and grit, and with an army of your people by your side. I pray that you will always remember that you, too, can be a sword.

Verses for When Everything Feels Impossible

As iron sharpens iron, so one person sharpens another. (Proverbs 27:17 NIV)

Consider it pure joy, my brothers and sisters, whenever you face trials of many kinds, because you know that the testing of your faith produces perseverance. Let perseverance finish its work, so that you may be mature and complete, not lacking anything. (James 1:2–4 NIV)

Questions for When Everything Feels Impossible

- What is the worst thing that could happen by trying something new?
- When you exercise regularly, do you typically see more results from a hard workout or an easy one?
- What have you gone through in life that was difficult but made you stronger? How can you apply that same thinking to what you are going through now?

Now, grab your sword and dance that dance of resilience.

10

WHEN YOUR PATH FEELS LONG

Seldom Are Our Paths Straight

I still remember the day I met Michael for the first time. I'd unassumingly made my way into a vast Tennessee auditorium and was standing quietly in the corner as he was introduced to an audience of hundreds. I had worked at this facility for a few years, but he was new. As he grabbed the microphone that day, I remember the look in his eyes, a gentle yet confident gaze that met the crowd seated before him. I was immediately drawn in.

After a brief introduction, he started sharing a story. It was a story that Dan had told often at work, so it was familiar to me, but this was the first time I'd heard Michael share it. Tears filled his eyes as he recalled aloud the details of the car accident that had claimed his sister Tiffany's life. I remember the way his voice shook, and the way his words seemed to linger in the air. And notably, the looks on the faces of those who took in his heartfelt plea. Twenty-five years before this moment, a drunk driver had taken the life of Michael's sister, but thanks to Michael's bravery and vulnerability that day, maybe some in this crowd would choose not to drive after drinking.

Michael was one of our new leaders onsite, and it was my responsibility to help him with his communication with the team and the community. As such, we started working together often. And as we started working together, I could barely articulate the feelings that were swirling through me. I was feeling something, but I couldn't find a label to describe those feelings. Admittedly, I pushed them aside to focus on work. Our relationship was professional, and it needed to stay that way.

I did know that I, and many others, immediately respected Michael's leadership style. He was kind but firm. Confident in his decisions yet inquisitive about perspectives. His silly energy was contagious, and even though I didn't yet know what I was feeling, I did know that I wanted to be around him as much as possible.

At the time I met Michael, we were both navigating failing marriages. As I've described in other chapters, I was far from being in a good place. I was confused, scared, and lonely—and at first, Michael's presence only complicated those feelings. But eventually, he became my clarity. Several months later, I still remember the day I went on one of my infamous walks and called him crying, so unsure of what the future would hold or how I would find my place again after the divorce. After listening to my worries, quietly and confidently he told me, "Courtney, just jump. I will catch you."

As my feelings for Michael intensified and I was finally able to articulate the realness of them, I was momentarily stopped by the thought that this was not the right time to enter into a new relationship, let alone one with a significantly older man who already had children and who just so happened to be my colleague.

Truthfully, Michael felt like the antagonist to all the ways I had previously and meticulously scripted and planned my life. But he also felt like a magnet. A magnet I could not, and did not want to, pull away from.

A good friend of mine at the time knew my situation well, and she could tell that I was struggling to accept my feelings for Michael. One day at work, she pulled me aside and told me she hoped I would not pass up such a special thing just because I was worried about the timing of it all. She reminded me that rarely do we get to perfectly plan and time our lives and that it would be a shame to let go of something that made me so happy.

So, after a while, I worked up the courage to let go. I let go of the fear of what my life would look like to other people, what they would think, or how they would react. I let go of trying to figure out what something should or should not be. And when I let go, I jumped. I jumped into a relationship that was just for me, no one else. A relationship with a man that made little-to-no logical sense but made my heart and soul come alive in ways I'd never experienced before.

And, as promised, Michael caught me.

I've talked a lot about the turbulence, resistance, and obstacles Michael and I had to overcome, but those challenges are partially what made us so strong and grateful for the love we share. The more opposition that came against us, the better we learned to hold on to one another and, more importantly, to God. And I firmly believe that those challenges were manageable because of the foundation we agreed upon.

During one of our first dates, Michael and I had a long and purposeful conversation. Having both come from failed marriages, it may have seemed obvious, but we did not want to be in a similar situation ever again. So we asked ourselves, *What must be true for this relationship to be lifelong? How can we both do better and be better, given a second chance?*

Our answer is what we call "our foundation," and this foundation was built on three key things: God. Communication. Trust.

First and foremost, we built our relationship on *God*. Michael was the first man I ever prayed with, attended church with, or even read the Bible with. And now we are doing our best to live a Christ-centered life, one that inspires our son to do the same.

The next part of the foundation is *communication*. We talk a lot. Even when we do not feel like it. You would be amazed at how much we are able to solve by just talking with each other. More importantly, we listen.

And finally, we have *trust*. Trust that we will always do right by each other. And trust that no matter what, we have each other's best interest at heart.

To this day, if Michael and I ever feel like we are getting off course, we remember our foundation and focus on those three things—God, communication, and trust—to help us stand tall again.

After the foundation of our relationship had been established and after about a year of dating, Michael asked my dad for his permission to marry me. He pulled my dad aside at my brother Ryan and sister-in-law Cristy's wedding and, thankfully, Dad gave him his blessing.

About a month later, Michael and I had a trip planned to Donner Lake in California, a place that has special meaning to our family. On October 10, early in the morning before the sun made its way through the clouds, Michael and I drove up the winding mountain road to the same spot that he and his sister, Tiffany, had visited decades prior. As he reminisced about his time there with his family as a kid, he put the car in park and asked me if I wanted to climb up the rocks just adjacent to the parking lot so that we could get a better view of the lake.

I was freezing, so part of me wanted to say no and stay in the warmth of the car. But the other part of me was mildly intrigued by the idea of an early picturesque moment at the top of this serene mountain. And admittedly, maybe I also had a feeling that a proposal was on its way.

So out of the car, over the rocks, and to the very top we went. We were sitting there taking in the view on one of the most beautiful mornings I have ever witnessed. The lake looked like glass, the clouds felt like they were mere inches above our heads, I had my arms looped through Michael's, and my head rested on his shoulder. I tried my best to be present, but truthfully, I was anxious because I was still anticipating a proposal. And boy, did I want it. We continued to sit there and take in the view for what felt like forever.

And then, in the least romantic way possible, Michael asked if I wanted a snack. As he offered me a piece of his granola bar, I started to think that maybe I was wrong. Maybe this really was not about a proposal and was just a scenic drive to start our vacation.

Sharply declining his offer for food, I turned around and was surprised to see Michael down on one knee holding a ring box in his hands.

I do not remember everything he said at that moment, but I do remember how he initially made the connection between the road we had just driven and our unique journeys that had led us to this moment. He talked about how neither had been straight or necessarily easy paths. He explained how sometimes, we could not always see clearly where we were heading, but that at times we just had to trust and keep moving forward. And lastly, he admitted that neither trek had been easy, but affirmed what I already knew—that both were undoubtedly worthwhile.

I can still remember what it felt like to wrap my arms around him and say yes that morning. It felt like nirvana. Even today, when I find myself needing to take my mind to a better place, I close my eyes and picture Michael and I standing at the top of that mountain. I picture the way the sun felt on my face, how the view looked, and the joy we both felt.

We spent the rest of the week celebrating all over California. We explored, ate, and drank our way through Lake Tahoe, Napa, and Sonoma Valley— and it was perfect. Shortly after the engagement, we planned a small and intimate wedding at Michael's parents' church just outside of Knoxville. At the same time, we also knew we wanted to start a family together. Despite our best efforts to plan and figure out the future, we instead returned to our commitment

to our foundation—and gave the fruition of our preg-
nancy and its timing to God.

Our wedding took place on a cold day in April.
My son was eight weeks old, inside my belly. That
morning, my father-in-law, Russ, drove me in his yel-
low Chevy Corvette to get my hair and makeup done,
and afterward, just he and I ate lunch together. After
our meal, Russ drove me back to the church and I sat
there in the quiet darkness of the church office and
prayed to God.

I thanked Him for a second chance. For a love that
was greater than I had ever imagined possible. I prayed
that I would never take for granted the mercy and love
God had shown me, and that I would do my best to
build a marriage and life that always honored Him.

After a few hours alone, it was time for me to get
dressed. Unlike my previous wedding, I did not want
a bridal party or a big fuss getting ready. I wanted all
my attention and energy that day to be focused on one
thing: my marriage to Michael. And it was. But that
didn't stop excitement from forming in my heart when I
heard a gentle knock on the other side of the door.

It was Gina. My close friend, the one who led me
out of the darkness during my divorce.

She came into the room, prayed with me, and
handed me a small gift. Shortly after, my dad came
and got me and it was time to walk down the aisle. He

and I stood quietly behind closed doors as the organist started playing "Ave Maria," a favorite song of my late grandmother's. Once again, her absence would be felt, but on this day it was different. Both tears and laughter filled the room as I walked down the aisle to Michael, holding lightly and confidently to my dad's arm.

Fewer than thirty people sat in the chapel that afternoon. There were no extravagant details planned for this day, and in the absence of those details were hours filled with the purest, most joyful love either of us could ever ask for. As we stood at the altar a few feet from those who loved us most and Pastor Steve asked us to read our vows to each other, I jokingly made Michael go first. I thought there was no way this engineer could out-write or out-speak me, a communications professional.

Boy, was I wrong.

Michael took the air from my lungs, as he read out loud the vows he'd written to me:

> We seldom find straight paths for our lives. As we journey through life, we go through twists and turns, hit dead ends and turn around, or take the wrong turn and wander lost for a while until we rejoin the path.
>
> We have tried so many times to perfectly plan what our path would look like, and time and time again we find God whispering, "I've got this."

Proverbs 3:5–6 says, "Trust in the Lord with all your heart and lean not on your own understanding; in all ways submit to Him and He will direct your paths."

Courtney Ann, our paths were always meant to join together, and here we are today celebrating our amazing journey together with family and friends.

They say love endures forever. You are the love of my life, and you are my forever.

Thank you, Michael. For everything you are.

Dear Little Bee,

Too often in life, we get caught up in thinking that our paths are always straight and allow ourselves to default to the easiest ones. The journey that led me to your father was not an easy one, nor was it straight or even traditional, by some standards.

But there is not a day that goes by that I am not grateful. Grateful for a God who gave us both a second chance, and for the love that has filled my heart and our home ever since.

My hope is that you grow up witnessing this love and choose to never settle for anything less. Your forever love does not need to look exactly like the love your dad and I share, but it needs to fill your soul in ways you never thought imaginable.

I want you to find a love that makes you want to get up every morning. A love that makes you want every minute to pass by a little slower. A love that leaves you wanting more. More time together, more hugs, more kisses to share. A love that makes you want to never let go of the other person's hand.

That is the kind of love I envision for your life.

And whether it is the pursuit of finding that love, or anything else in this world, do not waste a minute being discouraged if your path feels long. Or if it feels uphill, or like a winding road. You may not always find yourself where you want to be, but never lose sight of how far you have come.

Even if you need to stop and start over again.

Don't be discouraged. The hardest journeys often lead us to the most worthwhile places. Don't worry about making your path straight, just make it worth it.

Regardless of where your paths take you, know that there is a God who is directing your steps. And a mom and dad who are here, always, cheering you on.

Walk bravely, Little Bee.

Verses for When Your Path Feels Long

On the way of wisdom I direct you, I lead you on straight paths. (Proverbs 4:11 NABRE)

Make known to me your ways LORD; teach me your paths. (Psalm 25:4 NABRE)

Questions for When Your Path Feels Long

- Has there ever been a time in your life where you felt like the path was long or difficult? Maybe one where you had to start over?
- What was the result of that journey? What did you learn?
- What would you tell someone you love who is experiencing something similar now?
- If you've ever climbed a mountain or a hill, what was the view like from the top? How would you have seen or appreciated the view without the climb?

The best dances are the ones worth waiting for.

11

WHEN YOU HAVE TO START OVER

Our God Is a God of Second Chances

Let's rewind a little.

When Michael and I lived in Tennessee, we spent most weekends visiting his parents, Russ and Geni, at the lake. Early on, we planned a weekend where we'd spend a few days with Michael's parents together, and then I would stay with his parents while he traveled to Michigan.

This was still relatively early on in my relationship with Michael, so I was a little nervous about being by myself with Russ and Geni, even though I already loved them so much. On the Saturday night of my stay, they asked if I wanted to go to church with them the next morning. I could tell they were unsure of what I would say, because we hadn't talked a lot about faith at this point, but it was an easy yes for me. I'd already heard so many stories about their church and what it meant to them, including how they volunteered their time there, and how they even had a pew dedicated to their daughter, Tiffany.

Early that Sunday, we drove fifteen minutes down the road to the Community Church at Tellico Village for the morning service. As we made our way into the chapel, Russ introduced me to everyone as his future daughter-in-law. Geni stood by, quietly smiling, and I tried to contain my excitement. At one point I excused myself so I could go into the bathroom just to text my aunt Missy and tell her what was going on. Michael and I weren't engaged yet, so Russ and Geni's early affirmation elated me.

As the organist began to play, we made our way down the long aisle to the wooden pew marked in memory of Tiffany Youngs. As I looked toward the front of the church, I saw the organ pipes, beautifully lit with shades of purple and red, just like Russ had described. We quietly took our seats, with Russ seated between Geni and me.

As service began, Reverend Dr. Steve Prevatte stood behind the altar and led the congregation in prayer. Russ and Geni had hoped it would be him leading service that day, and I could tell they were excited that this was indeed the case. Pastor Steve had a Southern drawl and a gentle but confident demeanor about him, and it was very clear that he also had the love and respect of those he was serving that day. It was immediately easy to see why. Even from fifty feet away, I felt comforted by him.

Now, fast-forward a few years, when the time had come for Michael and me to choose a church to get married in and a pastor to marry us. It was an easy and heartfelt decision. Michael and I very much wanted to be married at his parents' church, and we prayed that Pastor Steve would be the one to officiate our ceremony. We were nervous to ask, because we recognized that while he knew Russ and Geni well, he did not know us at all. With quick prayers and crossed fingers, we made the ask. Thankfully, and much to our relief, he said yes.

But first, the church secretary told us, we needed to attend the required four weeks of premarital counseling. I'd never been through marriage counseling before, so I had no idea what it was or what we could expect. Nervously, I scheduled our first appointment for the coming month.

As part of this counseling, I did know it was inevitable that we would have to talk to Pastor Steve about our past divorces. I was always insecure about telling people I'd been married and divorced, but it was nothing compared to the anxiety I felt at having to admit this truth to a religious leader. For weeks I agonized about what I would say, how I would say it, and how it would be received.

It sounds silly, but I felt like for Michael it was different. Unfortunately, it is not that uncommon for people to get divorced and remarried at his age, but it definitely felt far less common for someone in their early thirties. Regardless of age, I knew that divorce was wrong and, in many cases, frowned upon in the church, and I was terrified that my truth would change Pastor Steve's opinion of us—and his willingness to marry us.

On the day of our first meeting with Pastor Steve, Michael came home from work and we took the video call together from our kitchen table. I nervously held Michael's hand and did my best to stay calm as Pastor Steve joined the call. But inside I was a nervous ball of anxiety with sweaty palms, and I just wanted to get the truth out there and over with.

We started the call with the normal pleasantries and getting-to-know-each-other small talk. Things like favorite sports teams and TV shows, and where our families were from. It was an easy enough way to get started, but I was still sweating in anticipation of the inevitable moment to come.

Then it happened. Pastor Steve asked Michael if he had been previously married, and before I knew it, I stepped in to say that actually we both had been married before. I could barely believe how quickly those words came flying out of my mouth. I think I shocked Michael too. However, it was too late to go back. I held my breath and braced for impact.

Without pause, Pastor Steve smiled and said, "Well, isn't it a beautiful thing that our God is a God of second chances? This is wonderful!" I almost fell off my chair. Had he really just said that? And did he really mean it?

He did. And this became a major turning point in how I viewed myself and my past. Truthfully, I was still healing from my divorce, and I definitely still struggled with guilt and shame when I spent too long thinking about it. I was repeatedly told that our God is a God of forgiveness, and I believed that when it came to everyone else, but for some reason I could not believe it for myself. I struggled to accept His forgiveness just as much as I struggled to forgive myself.

But Pastor Steve changed that. And I can't fully explain why. If I had to guess, I would say it was something about the quickness, gentleness, and confidence with which he responded to our past. I would like to believe it was God speaking through him, directly to me, at that moment.

It might sound cliché, but it felt as if someone had come in and lovingly lifted the heaviest weight off my chest. I felt light and warmth from within, and for the first time since my divorce, I felt forgiven. Not only by God, but by myself.

I finally accepted what many had tried to show me all along—that God's forgiveness, mercy, and grace are new every day, and that this is what makes the world so beautiful. It felt amazing to finally embrace this for myself.

What made this moment even more significant for me was that it was the first time I could ever recall being completely comfortable with any religious leader. I always felt like the church and its leaders expected perfection. I believed that my sins, divorce included, would only be frowned upon. I was afraid to be honest. I believed I had to hide the less-than-perfect parts of myself from the church or anyone closely associated with it, or I would be rejected and judged. But with Pastor Steve, I immediately felt safe and welcomed. In a single conversation, he embodied everything I had hoped to find in someone who led a church and its people.

Our premarital counseling continued for several weeks, and I found myself sincerely looking forward to every discussion. It never felt uncomfortable or like work. Quite the opposite, it felt clarifying and comforting. Pastor Steve was human and relatable. He helped Michael and I learn more about each other, our families, and our faith. He helped us begin to learn more about the kind of marriage that honored God and how we could work to maintain that. He even spent one-on-one time with me helping me with my anxieties and my own self-healing. Before our time with Pastor Steve, I never fully understood the power or intent of premarital counseling, but after we completed our sessions, the benefits were impossible to ignore.

On the day I married Michael, it felt like we had a friend and pastor standing between us at the altar, and it seemed like we'd known Pastor Steve our entire lives. Even though we'd met as complete strangers, he reached out his hand and walked alongside us on one of the most critical and formative journeys of our relationship. For that, and for so much more, I will always be grateful to him.

I felt strongly that I did not want our relationship with Pastor Steve to end after our wedding. And it hasn't. Thankfully, we have maintained contact with him, and every time we visit Michael's parents in Tennessee, we always try to see him and attend one of his sermons.

One of the best moments was the day we were able to introduce our son to him. Pastor Steve smiled, quickly reached out for our little boy, and held him in his arms as he greeted church attendees in his lobby. It might sound silly, but I think even my six-month-old son felt how special he was.

I often wonder if Pastor Steve will ever realize the profound impact he had on me, my marriage, and as a result, my son's life. I pray that he does.

Thank you from the bottom of my heart, Pastor Steve.

Dear Little Bee,

Please don't make the mistake I did and believe that our God and His disciples demand perfection from you, because quite frankly, the opposite is true. So often we tend to hide from the church when we sin or fall short of perfection, but the truth is we should find a church who makes us want to run toward it during these moments, not away.

If you find yourself in a position where you haven't found this kind of church, keep looking. I promise it is out there. But church isn't just a building you go to once a week on Sundays. Church is a body of people who remind you and show you the goodness of God's love. Find these people and love these people with all your heart.

If you ever find yourself in a situation where you feel like you made a mistake or screwed up, just remember I've been there too—we all have.

But most importantly, remember that our God is a God of second chances. I tend to believe He's also a God of third, fourth, and fifth chances, if we want them. Repent and try again, Little Bee.

The grace God shows you and me is the same grace we should extend to others. Just as much as I want you to assume goodness from people, I want you to also allow your heart to forgive. It might not always feel like the other person deserves it, but I promise you, it is worth a try. Especially if that person is yourself.

Lastly, when you meet people who remind you of God's Word and truth, hold tightly to them.

Verses for When You Have to Start Over

Forget the former things; do not dwell on the past. See, I am doing a new thing! (Isaiah 43:18–19 NIV)

Therefore, if anyone is in Christ, he is a new creation. The old has passed away; behold, the new has come. (2 Corinthians 5:17 ESV)

Questions for When You Have to Start Over

- Is there a part of your past that you feel shame and anxiety about?
- How would you feel if you asked for—and accepted—God's forgiveness instead?
- How would you feel if you forgave yourself? What is stopping you from doing this?
- How do you treat people you love who make mistakes, or who find themselves in a position to start over?

Sometimes, the second dance is even better than the first.

PART THREE

YOUR
FLIGHT

12

WHEN YOU THINK YOU NEED ALL THE ANSWERS

Intelligence Is Guided by Experience

In loving memory of Tiffany Youngs

Long before I ever met Michael, Dan, the man I worked for in human resources and labor relations, would tell me stories about Russ Youngs, a former plant director at our company (and my future father-in-law) and the time they'd spent working together in Oklahoma. Dan told me how much people admired and respected Russ, and frequently recalled positive attributes of his leadership. It was clear that Russ had created a legacy in our company that left an impression on many. He'd spent decades as a leader in manufacturing and, according to Dan, he was one of the toughest yet kindest managers he'd ever worked for.

Also according to Dan, Russ was known for his attention to detail that kept even the best of them on their toes. Since getting to know him myself, I can absolutely confirm that this is still one the most respected qualities about him.

But perhaps what Russ is most remembered for, and what Dan spoke the most fondly about, was the compassion and empathy he always showed everyone, particularly after the tragic death of his daughter, Tiffany, in 1996.

In fact, this is how I first learned about Russ and his family. It was during a safe driving discussion at work when Dan first shared this story with me.

Russ and Geni lost their daughter when she was only twenty years old. From the memories that have been shared with me, I know that Tiffany was an incredibly intelligent, witty, and caring young woman who was loved deeply by her family and friends. A former member of her high school debate team, she was actively pursuing a law degree at Texas Christian University. Tiffany was passionate about children and was often the best-dressed for any occasion.

When Dan first told me the story, he talked about the years that followed Tiffany's death. As Russ worked through his own pain, he would go and sit with anyone he learned was also grieving the loss of a loved one, if only to be nothing more than a shoulder to lean on and a comforting friend. He prioritized this above many other leadership obligations, because his people and their well-being were what always mattered most. It was a story that was told to me often, and it was rare that Dan could recall the details of Russ's selflessness and empathy without tears in his eyes.

When I first heard these stories, I did not know Michael, and I certainly never would have guessed that he would later move to Tennessee and eventually become my husband.

But he did. And when Michael and I did eventually meet and started dating, he, too, shared his own stories about Tiffany, Russ, and Geni. Michael painfully recalled the night he learned of Tiffany's death and what it felt like to go home and find his parents lying pain-stricken on the living room floor. But he also shared the happy memories of his sister, like when she would cover for him at dinner and eat whatever it was that he didn't like. (By the way, he's still an annoyingly picky eater.) Or the time when she went to her first dance, and Michael and Russ stood at the front door just to try to intimidate the guy who was taking her.

Michael frequently talked about Geni's kindness and big heart and Russ's passion for leadership and his family. When he spoke about his parents' marriage and how he admired the life they'd created together, it was very clear to me just how much of an influence they'd had on him and how much he adored and respected them.

These stories made me feel like I knew both of Michael's parents so well. Yet I still hadn't met either of them. And truthfully, it was months after Michael and I had started dating before they ever learned of my existence. It wasn't because we were hiding our relationship; it was because we were both incredibly nervous about telling his parents. We weren't sure how or when to tell them about our relationship. We were anxious about how they would react, given our age difference and the fact that both of us had recently separated from our previous spouses.

For weeks, we contemplated the timing of when to tell them. Admittedly, I started to get frustrated and impatient, and Michael did his best to reassure me that the right time was coming. And then one day, with no advance warning, Michael marched into my apartment and told me he'd finally worked up the courage to tell his parents about me, and that we were both invited to their home the following weekend.

Cue the sweaty palms and racing thoughts. Oh, and definitely the obsessive preparation.

After nervously and excitedly calling my family and friends to tell them what was happening, I immediately went shopping, bought a new outfit, and listened to several popular Republican podcast episodes just so I could feel somewhat prepared, knowing how much Russ loved to talk Republican politics and how little I knew about the topic.

A week later, Michael and I packed our bags and started the drive to his parents' home just outside of

Knoxville, Tennessee. The trip took a little over three hours, and with every painstakingly slow minute that passed, my nerves and anxiety climbed. And let me just say, Michael found it all completely amusing. Particularly when we pulled into their neighborhood and he decided to turn off the on-screen navigation so I couldn't tell how close we were getting.

As we drove the winding roads toward their home, I was completely blown away by the views of the mountains and lake. It was breathtaking and almost kept my mind off the upcoming introduction. *Almost.* For some reason, the weight of this introduction felt like none I'd ever experienced before. By this point, I knew that Michael was my forever person, and I was praying that by some chance, his parents would see it too. But somehow, it felt even bigger than that. I'd heard so many stories about Russ and Geni, and I feared I would fall short of their expectations. I worried that I would seem like an outsider who couldn't fit in or hold her own.

As we pulled into their driveway, I saw Russ and Geni standing side by side at their front door, holding hands like they always do. As soon as they saw us, they smiled and waved.

Michael put the truck in park.

Here goes nothing, I thought.

I quickly wiped the sweat off my palms one last time, took a deep breath, and, as confidently as I could, climbed out of the truck and walked toward two strangers who instantly felt like home. Despite my fears, the smile on my face came easily. I made my way to their front door and embraced them both in a hug. But, of course, it wasn't without me first stepping on Geni's toes. Try as I might, I will never fully escape my awkwardness.

As we went inside, I took in their beautiful home, the crystal chandelier, the grandfather clock, and, of course, the breathtaking view of the lake. Their home matched the way I'd heard both of them described—grand and warm.

I kept telling myself to breathe and relax. That only got me so far. Thankfully, by the grace of God, Russ immediately poured me a generous glass of wine that helped with those efforts. (When all else fails, sometimes you need a good glass of wine.)

We stood there chatting for a while, and what I remember most about that experience was the look in Russ's eyes. It was the same compassion and light I'd seen in Michael's eyes the first time I'd met him. I instantly felt comfortable—and, admittedly, somewhat further intimidated. The rest of the night was filled with effortless conversation, a lot more wine, plates of Geni's delicious seafood gumbo, and even a comical, and now infamous, power outage.

That night was the start of what has come to be hundreds of amazing conversations I've since shared with Russ. I find him to be one of the easiest and most enjoyable people I've ever talked with. He is both passionate about and interested in every conversation.

To this day, what I love most about our talks is the banter and laughter that often accompanies them. Sometimes we get going and can't stop. It's not uncommon for Geni and Michael to leave Russ and me at the table talking long after a meal has been finished. But I also love how my conversations with Russ regularly challenge and inspire me. They leave me wanting to learn and to know more. In fact, in the relatively short time I have known Russ, he has imparted more wisdom on me than most people I've known for decades.

Normally, interacting with someone as intelligent as Russ would make me incredibly insecure. I would feel a self-imposed pressure to have all of the answers and to know just as much about a topic as he does, just to feel like I could hold my own in the conversation. Because the truth is, I have never felt very smart. I wasn't anywhere near the top of my class in high school, and I only managed to get good grades in college because I worked harder than I ever had before as a result of being scared to death of failing and not being able to get a good job.

In my professional life, I'd used that same work ethic to help myself believe I deserved to be where I was. But deep down, I knew nothing came naturally to me. And that self-awareness had resulted in a lack of confidence.

But Russ helped change that.

During our earlier conversations, there were plenty of times when I would start to feel intimidated by Russ's seemingly endless amount of knowledge. But when I acknowledged this happening, he would casually respond with one of his favorite phrases that he'd learned from one of his favorite political commentators, Rush Limbaugh: "It's just my intelligence guided by my experience."

The first time I heard him say this, I remember taking his flippant response very literally. Naturally, his life had been filled with experiences that had helped him learn a lot. But what I have since realized is that the sarcasm and levity of his response was much more a reflection of the humility and empathy others had described before I even met him.

In all the conversations I've had with Russ, he never once has made me feel insecure or incapable. In fact, it's the complete opposite. Our conversations regularly empower and energize me, if I let them.

Russ has taught me that true knowledge is something that is acquired, not given. And that not knowing an answer is simply an exciting opportunity to learn more, not an excuse to shy away from a conversation. He's also shown me that true generosity is using what you've learned and experienced to help others. Even if it was the worst day of your life.

Russ's favorite phrase helped me to believe that I didn't have to come to the table equipped with all the answers I needed to be confident or to succeed. Instead,

I just had to be willing, humble, and patient enough to experience life and acquire knowledge along the way.

Russ helped me to decide that I was going to do my best to spend more energy focusing on what I did know, rather than what I thought I didn't. If experience was the true teacher in life, then I was already far more equipped than I'd given myself credit for, and I was just getting started.

At the young age of seventy-something, Russ is still learning. Every day. He is still actively pursuing experiences as a means of finding answers and gathering intelligence. And while I may never solve a math problem as fast as he does or hold my own quite the same in a political debate, I hope to at least emulate his passion for learning and for helping people.

Thank you, Russ and Geni. Not just for the incredible son and daughter you raised, but for the love and light you have brought to my life.

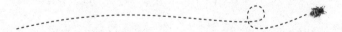

Dear Little Bee,

My hope is that you start from a place of humble confidence grounded in the knowledge that all you have experienced in your lifetime has uniquely equipped and prepared you.

This is a solid foundation, one that you can—and should—build upon.

The only way to keep building is to live your entire life with the attitude of a learner. Never think you're past the point of learning something new or that you have all the answers. Because you don't.

Every day, every moment, and every conversation is making you wiser, if you let it. So don't fret over what you think you don't know, because it's very possible that you're only one experience away from figuring it out.

And once you've figured it out—or, at the very least, experienced something—look for ways to use what you've learned to help others. Even your most painful moments can be opportunities to show love and kindness to those around you.

For months I heard stories about your Papa, his family, and his legacy. It feels nothing short of an honor to now be a part of it all and continue that legacy with you.

Verses for When You Think You Need All the Answers

I can do all things through Christ who strengthens me. (Philippians 4:13 NKJV)

The intention of the human heart is deep water, but the intelligent draw it forth. (Proverbs 20:5 NABRE)

Questions for When You Think
You Need All the Answers

- What experiences have you had that have taught you the most?
- From those experiences, what perspective and knowledge do you have that you could share with others?
- What is something you would like to know more about?
- How does learning something new make you feel?

The more you dance, the better you get.

13

WHEN YOU GIVE

Love Beyond Your Means

When I was growing up, it seemed completely normal to me that my mom worked multiple jobs. In middle school and high school, I remember a typical day beginning with my mom waking up between four and five in the morning, taking care of our animals, and then driving a few miles down the road to work at a horse barn, where she cleaned stalls and fed and watered more than ten horses before the sun rose. After this work was finished, she would drive back home to quickly shower and get ready for her full-time job as a receptionist at a veterinarian's office. Most of the time, she was headed to the office before I even woke up.

After she worked a regular eight-hour day at the vet's office, my mom would return home, change her clothes, and head back to the horse barn to repeat the morning's chores. She did this almost every day of the year.

In so many ways, she seemed invincible.

Mom also has always had an undeniable attention to detail. One of my favorite childhood memories was when she made me a horse-themed valentine box in which I could collect cards and candy during my school Valentine's Day party. I still remember her absolutely perfect execution of this project. She took a shoebox, cut six holes in it for a stuffed horse's legs, tail, and head to poke through, and covered the box with brown fur to complete the project. I felt like the coolest girl in school that day. The other kids had their basic Crayola-and-craft-paper valentine boxes, but I had a masterpiece.

My mom and I were close during these years. We had a strong bond that had been formed and held together through our shared love of horses. We spent most weekends traveling the state to horse shows, and I knew without a doubt that every time I climbed into the saddle, I was making her proud. Yet somehow, I was oblivious to the fact that she was working tirelessly just so I could pursue my passion.

Like most "horse show moms," my mom worked hard, doing everything from bathing my horse and braiding its mane to making sure my show outfits were in perfect condition. And while she liked to say it was because I was spoiled, I would often argue back that showing horses was just as much for her as it was for me. Deep down, I bet she would agree. We were a team.

When I left for college, horses and horse shows were no longer a thing in my life. I sold my horse, donated most of my show clothes, and, eventually, my mom stopped working at the horse barn—a job she'd taken in order to pay for my hobby. When I look back at that period of my life, I remember it felt like a normal change of chapters for me. In hindsight, it really was the start of a much more significant change in our mother-daughter relationship.

Let me tell it to you straight. My mom and I endured a few hard years in our relationship once I left for college. If you asked me why, I honestly couldn't tell you, and I'm sure my memory would be different from hers. I just know it was hard for us. A lot of arguments, weeks passing without speaking. And judgments—a lot of judgments.

People think the teenage years are the toughest, but I think the early twenties are a strong contender. At least mine were. During those four years of college, I became bitter toward my mom. I seemed to find fault with her in just about anything I could. I'd previously admired her work ethic, but as I got older, I realized it was just as much a necessity as it was a characteristic. And that angered me. In so many ways, I realized just how much we'd been living beyond our means, and I imagined the stress that must have caused her. I both sympathized and hated the fact that she had been married and divorced three times, and, if I'm being completely honest, part of me judged her for that too.

Thankfully, as we get older, we learn to see the world differently. We learn that the world is much bigger, and far more complex, than our personal opinions. We learn that our parents are human beings who are just doing the best they can with what they have, and that they deserve love and grace in all the same ways as anyone else. I guess you could say that experience is a beautiful way to gain perspective.

After a rocky few years, my mom and I found solid ground again, and it was thankfully during a time when I needed her most—when I was going through my own divorce.

Don't worry, the irony was not lost on me either.

My mom stepped in and stepped up when I needed her, without pause or hesitation. She offered perspective and advice, and, most importantly, she offered her unwavering support. With every tear-filled phone call—and there were a lot of them—she helped me get through it, one day at a time. I leaned on her, and she held me strong.

That is likely why my mom was one of the first people I told when I met Michael. I could barely contain my excitement on the day I called to tell her about him. I was driving home from work, and I couldn't wait to tell her about this man I'd met. I was both excited and nervous, and I made her promise that she wouldn't tell a soul. As soon as I put my car in park, I sent her a picture of Michael and made her swear she would delete it right away.

I didn't think for a second about how she would perceive the news, or what judgment she would have because of the age difference between Michael and me. I knew she would support me, because I knew she could tell how happy I was. And I was right—my mom embraced my new relationship with open arms and enthusiasm. So much enthusiasm that a few months later, she hopped on a plane and flew to Tennessee to meet him. Of course, they hit it off beautifully.

As much as I sometimes refuse to admit, I know my mom and I are a lot alike. But I will always be the first to remind her—and anyone else—that we also have a lot of differences. For instance, it's no secret that we often have a comedically horrible difference of opinion when it comes to money matters.

Allow me to explain.

For a lot of reasons outside of her control, my mom has never had it easy when it comes to finances. Hence the multiple jobs. Recently, she was running a little tight on money after some unexpected costs incurred with her vehicle. There is absolutely no shame in that; we've all been there. But imagine my surprise when four days later she called to tell me she was sending my son birthday presents in the mail. The logical side of my brain could not keep up.

I am what I would like to believe a predominantly logical thinker, especially when it comes to money. Needless to say, I was angry she was choosing to spend her extra money on gifts, even if they were for her beloved grandson. When she called, I truly could not believe her audacity.

It was not long after this that Michael and I were in church listening to a message focused on generosity. Holding my husband's hand, I listened intently to Pastor Craig Groeschel's words and prayed about what God was trying to tell me that day.

According to Pastor Craig, there are three qualities of generous people:

1. Generous people give *willingly*.
2. Generous people give *proportionately*.
3. Generous people give *sacrificially*.

Number three. The message found my heart with undeniable clarity. My mom had always been someone who gives sacrificially. It was never about money for her, no matter how much maybe it should be. It was always about bringing happiness to someone else.

She loves and gives beyond her means—sometimes at a detriment to herself—because that is just who she is. She is a generous and loving woman who wants more for others than she does for herself. I may not always immediately agree with it, but deep down I love her for it.

I did not have the foresight or maturity to see this when I was in college, but I see it now. She demonstrated this generosity during the years when she helped pay for my horse shows. And here she was, doing it again for my son.

Not only did this sermon challenge my harsh criticism of my mother, but it also reminded me that giving is an invitation to come closer to God. An invitation I am eager to accept, but one that doesn't come as naturally for me as it does for her.

I am embarrassed to admit this, but because I grew up seeing what it looked like to have financial struggles, I've often quickly dismissed any extra spending for fear it would put a strain on our household, even if we had more than enough to get us by. And unfortunately, donating to charities and giving money to other people often felt like extra spending to me.

Through Pastor Groeschel's sermon, I was reminded that being generous does not always make sense or feel safe. But it is exactly what we are called to do. So, Michael and I decided to work together to actively look for ways where we can help make a difference using what we've been blessed with. This includes regular donations to our church, local nonprofits, and community Bible studies.

Being irrationally generous does not always feel safe, but in the end, it does feel right.

Thanks, Mom.

Dear Little Bee,

I will never have your Gigi's eye for decorating or talent for craft projects, but I do hope to always emulate both her hard work and her selflessness. Even if I routinely tease her about her chickens, the truth is that I have never seen animals with a better life than the ones Gigi takes care of. Similarly, I have never witnessed a time when she was not trying to do good for anyone she loves.

While your dad and I will do our best to raise you to be fiscally responsible, I do want you to embrace loving beyond your means. Be kind and be irrationally generous. After all, we've been put on this earth to love one another. So love big, and love well.

I know it's likely inevitable that you will grow up and form opinions about what I did or did not do right for you in this lifetime. You will come to your own conclusions about how your dad and I raised you and every choice we made in between. I will do my best not to take your opinions too personally. But I am sensitive like Gigi, so take it easy on me.

Similarly, someday you might choose to become a parent yourself. And then we can revisit that list of judgments. Just kidding. Sort of.

But truthfully, I do want you to know that you and your wife will get to decide what to repeat or avoid with your own children. As you will see, it is a big decision. I will pray every day that your dad and I will show you an example of love, marriage, and family that is worth repeating. Even if not in its entirety.

Above all, and most importantly, Little Bee, I want you to know that you can always call your mom. I will always have your back. I am so proud and so lucky to call you my son, and although as I write this letter to you, you are not yet one year old, I can already tell you that you are, without a doubt, my pride and joy. The best thing I will ever do is love you. I love you forever.

Verses for When You Give

Give in proportion to what you have. Whatever you give is acceptable if you give it eagerly. And give according to what you have, not what you don't have. (2 Corinthians 8:11–12 NLT)

Jesus sat down near the collection box in the Temple and watched as the crowds dropped in their money. Many rich people put in large amounts. Then a poor widow came and dropped in two small coins. Jesus called his disciples to him and said, "I will tell you the truth, this poor widow has given more than all the others who are making contributions. For they gave a tiny part of their surplus, but she, poor as she is, has given everything she had to live on." (Mark 12:41–44 NLT)

Questions for When You Give

- What does being generous look like to you?
- Is what you are giving proportionate to what you are receiving?
- How can you be a blessing to someone else, using what you have been blessed with?

Sometimes, the dance is for someone else.

14

WHEN YOU AREN'T SURE
WHAT TO SAY OR DO

Choose Your Words, Time, and Energy Wisely

High school can be really tough, and sometimes it just plain sucks. If you, too, have made your way through these notorious four years, you might agree that the experience is just as tough as it is formative. Unfortunately, for most of us during those years, friends come and go and insecurities and unfair moments are a dime a dozen. Let us not forget the braces and the awkward height differences between most boys and girls.

When I think back to my own high school experience, it is not without mixed emotions. There are plenty of good memories, like homecoming dances with friends, traveling abroad, and playing on sports teams. But there are just as many difficult memories. Countless heartbreaks, friends who suddenly became enemies, an overwhelming desire to be independent long before I was actually ready, and a long list of things I am forever grateful I got away with. But somewhere in between all the good, bad, and chaotic are powerful learning moments. Even if you do not immediately realize it. And I'm not talking about the class material, although there is definitely a place for that. Except for me and algebra. That was not, and still is not, a thing.

What I am talking about are the moments that have the ability to shape your life. The moments that are handed to you by people who genuinely want to invest in you and your future. For me, one of the most significant lessons I learned was on a day when I was misbehaving in class with some friends and, rather than give me a well-deserved punishment, my teacher, Mr. Bertani, shared with me some timeless advice that has stuck with me throughout the years. In front of the entire classroom, he calmly but confidently told me that time and words were two things I could never take back. And quoting Lecrae, a well-known singer, he advised me to choose both resources wisely: "Don't use time or words carelessly. Neither can be retrieved."

There was a notable silence in the air and likely a confused but somewhat attentive expression on my face. No doubt Mr. Bertani used this advice as a warning that day. And no doubt his stern delivery was warranted. It made sense to me then, but it became clearer as the years went on. Because the words Mr. Bertani shared that day went miles beyond a cautionary advisement.

Mr. Bertani's words became a foundation for the years that followed. A constant reminder that the words I choose in every situation carry weight. I now see and believe that words have the ability to build someone up or tear them down. Throughout my life, I have witnessed how words can inspire, teach, and motivate us, just as they can also devastate, hurt, and divide us.

What I learned that day in Mr. Bertani's classroom was that there are a lot of factors that play into what the final impact of our words will be, but there is typically a common denominator: permanence. We can never unhear, unsee, or unfeel words that have been shared. Words are sent with a one-way ticket to the recipient. And as the sender, it is our responsibility to pause and think about what we're going to say before we say it. And that includes not just what we say to other people, but what we say to ourselves.

And then there is the resource of time, something that is not permanent and quite literally depletes with every second. There is no day that is granted the privilege of being lived twice. That is why what you choose to spend your time on, or who you choose to spend your time with, is so important.

It has been almost fifteen years since the day I heard this advice for the first time. Yet there has not been a period of my life since that hasn't been shaped by it in some way. And that is a gift and a lesson I never saw coming.

I've also been privileged to have friends that have taught me similar valuable lessons, like my friend Daisy. She and I met a few years ago as colleagues. As I write this, we've still never met in person, but Daisy has easily and beautifully forged a place in my heart and life.

I will admit that when I first met Daisy, I was incredibly intimidated. She is a beautiful, talented, and smart woman, not to mention someone with great eyebrows. Yet despite my immediate intimidation, I was drawn to her. In so many ways it felt like we'd known each other forever. I enjoyed working with her and learning from her, but I loved our developing friendship far more.

Slowly but surely, every time we talked I learned more about who she was and a bit more about where she was coming from. I knew she and her family had immigrated from Mexico when Daisy was very young, and that she had begun a career within the diversity, equity, and inclusion space because it was a topic she cared deeply about. But it was still early in our friendship, and there was clearly more for me to learn about her and her story.

Fast-forward several months to Hispanic Heritage Month, when Daisy found the courage to share more of her own story with our entire company. Her story, which she titled "Twenty-Five Years Later, I'm Stepping Out of the Shadows and Celebrating my Identity," shared some of the details of her family's migration to the United States, her experience as a Deferred Action for Childhood Arrivals (DACA) student, and how the two events helped to shape her identity over the nearly three decades that followed:

> *There was a time in my life where I wanted nothing more than to conceal my identity as a first-generation undocumented immigrant from Mexico. At that time, it felt imperative to my survival—and to that of my family's—that I camouflaged myself, compartmentalized my home and social life, and that under no circumstance did I attract any negative attention because of my immigration status.*
>
> *It's been nearly twenty-five years since my family immigrated to the United States. Now, more than ever, I understand the power that comes from embracing my whole identity. My upbringing, my lived experiences, and my heritage—which once made me feel ashamed—are precisely what make me equipped.*

Her *words*. They were so honest and powerful.

I remember reading this story like it was yesterday and being surprised by how much I didn't know about my friend. How many questions I'd left unasked and how much of an opportunity I had to learn more. I'd correctly guessed that her family's journey to the United States was an important part of her story, but I was definitely ignorant about the details and significance. Furthermore, until Daisy shared this part of her story with our team, I had a very narrow and extremely limited viewpoint on illegal immigration to the US. To be completely transparent, I once saw the issue very much as black-and-white. Or right and wrong, for that matter. However, I realized that much of my opinion had come from the words I'd heard.

In the media, the topic of illegal immigration to the US is polarizing. Parties on both sides use it as a pawn to divide so many of us. But Daisy was different. She used her words to show us the human side of the issue and to connect those of us who didn't think we needed to be connected. It is amazing how someone's choice of words can completely change someone else's perspective.

Just like in my other favorite friendships, Daisy challenged my viewpoint and, ultimately, very much changed my opinion. I quickly learned that there are layers to right and wrong, black-and-white. And within those layers are real humans, hard-earned experiences, moving stories, and much more to consider than what the latest media story might broadcast.

As the years went on, my conversations and friend-ship with Daisy only strengthened. We've become more vulnerable with each other, and although we come from two very different places, it has been amazing to see all the similarities we share. And, like most good girl-friends, our talks often head in the direction of our love lives—both in the past, present, and future.

Daisy is well aware of my own relationship journey, and she's kindly shared details of her own. Although we are coming from very different places—me, a divorced and remarried woman, and her, still actively dating in pursuit of her forever—it never takes us long to find common ground.

One of the major similarities we share is that we both have a somewhat unhealthy tendency to want to control, plan, and predict our lives. And with that control comes an even less productive habit of replaying and rewinding the past in our minds. It is an endless pursuit to understand what went wrong, what could have been done better, and why the hell we did not get it right the first time. It is one thing to know and believe God has a plan, but apparently it's a whole other level to choose not to overanalyze or predict it.

In one of our conversations, after several rounds of shed tears, a few laughs, and a never-ending promise to always be there for each other, we realized that each of us had a decision to make. Would we continue to invest ourselves in overanalyzing our pasts and trying to predict our futures? Or would we choose to invest all of that energy elsewhere?

Ultimately, we all have a limited amount of energy. Just like our time and our words, we must choose to spend our energy wisely, because we can never get it back. The more energy we choose to invest in replaying our pasts and trying to predict our life's outcomes, the less energy is available for us to enjoy the present—and future—moments of our lives. And the now and the forward are the most powerful and purposeful places.

I hung up the phone that day after my conversation with Daisy, unable to remove our conclusion from my heart. The next morning as I went for a run, it felt like the stories and words Daisy and I had shared were playing on repeat, echoing over and over within my own thoughts. My footsteps felt lighter. My heart felt fuller.

It is amazing how God and the universe can send—and often repeat—a message during the times when we need it most. It is even more amazing to see how God gifts us with unique friendships at the right time, in our own right place.

Thank you, Mr. Bertani, and my *alma gemela*, my twin soul, Daisy.

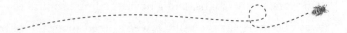

Dear Little Bee,

Time, words, and energy are three things you can never take back. For that reason alone, I will always caution you to choose them wisely.

Before you speak, take a moment to think about the words you're about to say. Your words are so powerful and will likely far outlast you. The facts of a situation may not be controllable, but your words are.

Before life passes you by, take a moment to consider how you are spending your time. Fill your days with things that bring happiness, love, and peace to your life and the lives of those around you. That does not necessarily mean always being busy, but it does mean being purposeful. It means making the time for things that matter most, like visiting family and spending time with loved ones.

As you choose how to spend your time, try not to get so hung up on asking yourself, Now what? Instead, enjoy your "now" and everything that moment brings. Especially if that moment brings you a perspective that can change your life for the better.

Choose to invest your energy in things that move you forward. Just like the proper foot placement on a fall morning run, where you decide to put your energy can either propel you forward or be wasted in unnecessary arm swings and flailing footsteps.

And lastly, Little Bee, please be kind and respectful to your high school teachers. They deserve your best.

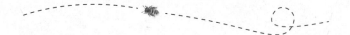

Verses for When You Aren't Sure What to Say or Do

Gracious words are like a honeycomb, sweet to the soul and healing to the bones. (Proverbs 16:24 NIVUK)

The words of one's mouth are deep waters, the spring of wisdom, a running brook. (Proverbs 18:4 NABRE)

Questions for When You Aren't Sure What to Say or Do

- How can you use your words to help or make some-one feel good?
- How can you spend your time today in a way that brings yourself or someone you love happiness?
- What areas of your life can you redirect your energy toward that would be more productive than where you are currently investing this resource?

Dance with intention.

15

WHEN YOU ARE FRUSTRATED WITH OTHER PEOPLE (OR WITH YOURSELF)

Assume Goodness

Life has taught me that sometimes, a seemingly insignificant moment can actually be a major life building block in disguise. This is a concept that's both exhilarating and terrifying all at once. I have learned that sometimes even the pair of shoes you choose can set the course for a life-shaping experience.

One of those experiences in my own life was the first day I wore high heels to a company function. For context, as a five-foot-nine woman, it was not—and still is not—often that I grab a pair of heels to complete an outfit. However, on this particular day, I was attending my first company function as an intern, and I wanted to make a great impression. I started with the most professional-looking outfit I owned, nude high heels included.

Oh, the bravery.

As I strutted through the front door of the down-town Detroit event space that evening, I felt confident with the impression I would be making. But panic soon set in when I learned I'd be playing in a table-tennis tournament with my selected partner, Tony, the company's senior vice president.

Neither the activity nor my partner complemented my footwear well. Forget the nerves that were unraveling because of Tony's title; the real panic set in because he was five feet six at best. I would be standing at least five inches above him, thanks to my high heels. It felt like the unwelcome return of one of my middle school dances. *Why, hello, my biggest insecurity—how I have missed you!*

After taking a deep breath and quickly wiping my sweaty palms on my outfit, I grabbed the paddle with a confidence that could only be mustered from deep within. A confidence built upon the many family Christmas parties that featured table-tennis matches in the basement of my family's home. As an intern, I may have been a stranger to the corporate world, but I was definitely no stranger to table tennis. And those two-inch heels were not about to stop me. Thankfully, my competitive nature far outweighed my nerves, because in addition to an impressive third place finish in the tournament, this seemingly odd matchup was also the start of a great mentorship in my life. Tony was the first senior vice president I ever worked for, and although his title put him far above me, he had the uncanny ability to make me feel like an equal.

As a junior employee, I felt at ease because of Tony's approachability and transparency, and his genuine interest in what I had to say and how I was doing made me respect him as a leader even more.

Tony made a habit of regularly meeting with team members on an individual basis, and not once did I dread or worry about these meetings. It was quite the opposite—I looked forward to our discussions every time. A fiery Italian who rarely left you guessing what he was thinking, Tony had an unapologetic demeanor that reminded me a little bit of home.

One thing I learned quickly about the automotive industry is that it is not for the faint of heart. It is a tough industry and often an emotional one. At one particular team meeting that Tony hosted early in my career, we gathered at an off-site location just north of Detroit. The meeting was scheduled during a time of particularly high tension within our company and industry. People were at odds. Work was stalled.

What I remember most about this day is that as Tony opened the meeting that morning, he acknowledged the period of tension we were in and immediately encouraged all of us to *first assume goodness and competence* with one another.

He took a long pause, as if he knew what he'd said had caught people by surprise. It was the first time I'd ever heard such a thing. It seemed so simple, yet felt so profound. Truthfully, I was surprised that Tony was approaching the situation in this way, probably because of his natural demeanor. He had a lot of fire in him. Especially if people disagreed with him.

After the initial shock of Tony's words wore off, my mind immediately jumped to all my notoriously hard-to-work-with colleagues by whom I was challenged daily. No way could Tony's advice apply to me or to them.

Advice dismissed. (At first.)

However, I respected Tony, and from that respect came an honest intention of wanting to hear and adhere to his advice. So, to the best of my ability, I set aside my own ego, and when I did, I started to realize just how much of a point Tony had. I took an honest look at my daily interactions in the workplace, like someone was holding a mirror up to my face. It was not hard to see that my default assumptions of how people were responding in difficult situations were often the complete opposite of what Tony was encouraging us to do. As it turned out, in most cases I wasn't assuming goodness or competence. I was *assigning labels* like ignorance, disrespect, or even vindictiveness. What I learned is that I was only limiting myself.

For instance, when I thought about how a coworker was acting difficult during a meeting or not agreeing with my approach, my first assumption was generally that they were just not easy to work with, or that they didn't respect my opinion or position. Often, I simply dismissed them as flat-out wrong.

The result was that I would often leave those meetings feeling emotional and subsequently spend the next thirty minutes (or more) venting about what had happened to anyone who would listen. I could barely concentrate on anything else. More often than not, it would bother me well into the evening hours, and I would even find myself still complaining about it the next day. In hindsight, I realize what an incredible waste of my time and energy this was.

Thinking about Tony's advice, I knew that I wanted, and quite frankly needed, to use both my time and energy differently if I wanted a successful and happy career. Most days I would have just settled for a sane one.

So, I decided that day that I wanted to be the type of person who did her best to first assume goodness and competence. I thought that if I could do this, even if just for a *fraction* more than I had been, the chances were high that I would gain back control of my emotions, relieve myself of such a restrictive mental burden, and ultimately use my time for good. As it turns out, it was never a matter of if I *could* do this; it was a matter of deciding that I *would*.

So, I can, and to the best of my ability, I do. Assuming goodness means that I now do my best to first recognize that everyone is invested and doing their best to get the job done. Just because someone disagrees with me or even acts unpleasant does not make them a bad or mean person. Maybe I'm stating the obvious here?

And assuming competence means that instead of immediately dismissing someone as wrong, I challenge myself to actively listen to what they are saying, without automatically formulating my response or opinion. After all, just because their approach may be different from mine does not make it wrong. Maybe it's even better.

Starting with these two simple tactics has given me the intellectual and emotional space to learn more, gain different perspectives, and feel better about the work I am doing on a daily basis. Perhaps the most rewarding part has been that I've been able to build even stronger relationships with the people I work with. That is something I value the most.

But this isn't just about the workplace. In fact, I think assuming goodness and competence is even more important in our personal lives. I recently realized just how much I was falling short in applying this mindset outside of work. And not just with family and friends, but also with complete strangers. For instance, there have been plenty of times when I'm at a grocery store, or grabbing a drink at a local bar, and the cashier or bartender appears unpleasant. My instinctive reaction is to judge the person and their perceived lack of friendliness, and then respond with a matched coldness. And it doesn't stop there. When someone doesn't smile back in the hallway, I think to myself, *What a grump! They must not be a nice person.* When someone cuts me off in traffic? *The audacity! They must be a really terrible driver.* When someone I love hurts my feelings? *They must not care about me.*

I would not necessarily label myself as a negative person, so it surprised me how quickly I jumped to these poor assumptions of people.

I don't think that I am completely alone in this either. Unfortunately, I think a lot of us have been conditioned to assume the worst about each other. Maybe it's a self-preservation thing, or maybe it's just how our brains are wired. But if you stop to think about it, that type of mindset can be a really sad way to live our lives. Exhausting too.

Tony's advice that day challenged me to not only think about my own actions and predispositions, but also to acknowledge the well-known truth of unseen struggles. In fact, I think we all need to be reminded that you never know what someone is going through behind closed doors.

The good news is that if you start from a place of assuming goodness, you automatically give grace for whatever someone may be dealing with. You give grace for someone who might just be having a bad day, or even a bad year. You give grace for someone who might be deeply insecure, or even frantically rushing to a hospital for their loved one. You give grace for your own loved ones by trusting that it was never their intention to hurt your feelings, and you give grace because they really do love you, and you them.

Simply put, you give grace because we are all humans who inherently fall short from time to time.

Grace is like a human superpower. When you assume goodness and competence and give grace, you have the power to make different and better choices. Choices like offering kindness to someone who may really need it that day, without an expectation of anything in return. That's something I think this world needs a little more of.

As I improved in my ability to assume goodness and competence, I realized that perhaps the most difficult person of all to give these positive assumptions to is ourselves.

We all mess up from time to time. We fall short. We get it wrong. We hurt someone we love. This is an inevitable and painful part of being human. Yet despite this known truth, it can be so difficult to give ourselves the same amount of grace that we give others. We think we know better, that we should be better. We expect perfection. We do things we never thought we would.

We get off course, fall down, and sometimes take a long time to get back up.

For all of these reasons and more, assuming goodness and competence first is a skill that our minds need to be constantly engaged with. It is easy to identify opportunities to do this after the fact, but it is intensely more powerful if we can apply it from the onset. Both for ourselves, and for the world around us.

Thank you, Tony.

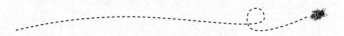

Dear Little Bee,

Here's the first thing I will tell you: always check an event's agenda before you go. Being prepared will set you apart. You never know how even a pair of shoes can change your life. And while I do not anticipate high heels being an issue for you, I would still encourage you to choose wisely.

Next, assuming goodness and competence is not a given; it is a choice. A choice I want you to make as often as you can.

Be aware of the labels you assign to others, to situations, and to yourself. Those labels carry a lot of weight and can easily change the way you experience life. Don't let negative labels weigh you down or limit your potential.

The truth is, sometimes people are being difficult because they're going through something difficult. Use your superpower. Be the person who gives them the grace they probably need. You never know who may need it most.

Smile and be kind, even when you do not always want to. Pray for others, even if you don't feel like it.

And lastly, don't be so hard on yourself. Let me fill you in on a little secret: you will not get it right 100 percent of the time, and no one expects you to—especially not me.

And here's one more thing to remember: there will be plenty of times in this life when the person who needs grace the most from you, is you.

A Verse for When You Are Frustrated with Other People (or with Yourself)

Above all, love each other deeply, because love covers over a multitude of sins. (1 Peter 4:8 NIV)

Questions for When You Are Frustrated with Other People (or with Yourself)

- When you think of a frustrating person in your life, what would it look and feel like if you assumed goodness and competence about them first?

- How do you react when someone is unfriendly to you?
- Thinking back on a time when you messed up or failed, did you give yourself grace? How would it feel if you did?
- How would you talk to a friend or someone you loved who made the same mistake you did?

Dance kindly.

16

WHEN YOU'RE FEELING OVERWHELMED

Give It to God

My brother, Ryan, and I have not always been as close as we are today. It took us a long time to recognize that while life made us siblings, it was our choice to become friends.

Growing up, I was what I would like to think of as a stereotypical little sister. I followed Ryan around every chance I got and considered myself twice as lucky if I could find ways to annoy both him and his friends. I often took his swift dismissals of my presence as personal pleas to hang around longer.

But, like most little sisters, I also admired the heck out of my big brother. He was the coolest person I knew, and he had both the confidence and independence I wanted for myself.

The older we got, the closer we became. We had so much fun together, and I think we both realized how much we had in common but also how much we had each other's backs. That loyalty and friendship did not change when I decided to move away from home.

In fact, after I moved to Michigan, Ryan and I only got closer. At the time, he was going through a particularly difficult relationship and we would talk a lot about what that looked and felt like for him. I remember feeling very special, because Ryan did not make a habit of letting a lot of people into his life. I valued that I was the exception. But as the years passed, there were moments when it felt like the opposite was happening. When instead of leaning on me for support, he was shielding me by pretending everything was okay and acting noticeably distant.

When I finally found the courage to ask him about it, I was somewhat surprised by his response. I'd been taking his silence and distance personally, when really, according to him, it was his way of protecting me and everyone else from what he was struggling with.

I should not have been surprised, because Ryan has always been a natural protector of our family. But I was also saddened. Not only was he struggling with his circumstances, but he was struggling with how he felt about himself. It was painful to realize that he couldn't see in himself the positive things that the rest of us saw in him.

My first impressions of my brother—dating back to when I was the annoying little sister—remained intact more than three decades later. He was still the coolest person I knew. Unapologetically himself, confident and capable. I wanted him to see that and believe it too. When Ryan told me he didn't want to bother or burden anyone, I told him that he was being ridiculous, that the people who loved him the most wanted to be let into his life. We wanted to stand by him and support him through all seasons of life—including the hard ones.

He somewhat humored my emotional plea, and we ended the call with a heartfelt "I love you." I hung up the phone feeling pretty good about the advice I'd given him. It was honest, and it felt like he'd needed it. Little did I know, once again, that perhaps the person who needed that advice the most was myself.

At this point, I'd been back to work for almost five months after having taken my maternity leave. To say I was struggling with the adjustment was a huge understatement. Despite all the warnings from people who loved me, I never saw what was coming.

Unlike some women, I didn't always know I wanted to be a mom. My career had always been a major part of my identity, and I doubted I'd ever have time for anything else. But when I met Michael, that changed. After my son was born, I spent six months dedicating almost every minute to him. It was beautiful, exhausting, and purpose-giving. Unlike most new parents, Michael and I did not have a lot of help close by. We had just moved to Missouri, where we barely knew anyone, and we were now hundreds of miles away from any family. Yet despite this, and even though it was all new to me, being a mom felt natural. Yes, there were definitely hard moments, but for the most part it was a truly enjoyable and happy time. And, much to my surprise, I felt good about this new identity and role of mine.

Becoming a mom brought a lot of clarity to my life. Before my son was born, I'd dreamed of writing a book. I'd actually started and stopped writing one several times throughout the years. I guess before I had him, the timing had never felt quite right. But one night when my son was just a few months old, I felt in my heart that God was calling me to start writing again. So I did. Almost every time my baby napped, I typed. I didn't know what the end result would be, but I didn't care. I was writing, and I was writing for him.

And then it was time for me to go back to work. Suddenly, my baby and I went from spending all our time together to me being grateful if we could be with each other for a few uninterrupted hours. I knew that this transition was inevitable, but I spent weeks grieving the change. It felt like I was closing a beautiful chapter in my life, and I wasn't fully ready. We were fortunate enough to have someone who could take care of him while I worked from home, so while it was great to be able to see my baby throughout the day, at times it felt like having a front-row seat to what I was missing most. And that was hard.

To complicate matters, I returned to work in yet another new position with my company. In this assignment, I was working in a new capacity for a high-profile and notoriously demanding leader who was leading the company through a very challenging time.

I felt like a rookie again. Everything felt ridiculously hard. I was angry at my job for taking me away from my baby, yet grateful I had a job to help provide for our family in the way I'd always envisioned. I wanted to be the same successful career woman I'd been before, and I also wanted to be a stay-at-home mom who only focused on her family. That was an identity crisis I'd never planned for.

And if that wasn't enough, I decided that writing and publishing the book I'd started was something that needed to happen. Fortunately, a publisher agreed. Which meant that for weeks, in between work obligations, I continued my writing. I would start writing as early as 4:30 a.m. to get in some writing time before my son woke up. I took hours of classes, developed content, and continued to write well into the evenings. Against all odds, my book was coming to fruition.

I was excited but also terrified at the idea of publishing a book. I felt out of my league most days, and even though a publisher was supporting me, I still questioned whether or not I could make it happen. And if I *could* make it happen, I doubted anyone would really be interested in reading my story.

Through all of this, I completely underestimated how difficult trying to balance my role as wife, mom, and career woman—and now, author—would be. When people cautioned me that being a working parent would be hard, I thought I'd be the exception. I wrongly assumed that returning to work and writing a book would just mean I'd need to get more done in a day, and that did not scare me a bit. I believed myself to be a master of productivity.

The problem was that it wasn't just the balancing act that was difficult. The most frustrating part about the entire thing was that most days, I felt like just an okay mom, an okay wife, an okay employee, and an okay writer. And being just okay was never fulfilling to me.

I wanted to be the kind of mom who made her son every meal from scratch, who was able to be fully present during every playtime. I wanted to be the kind of wife who always had the mental space for her husband, who had dinner ready on the table and a smile on her face every time he came home from work. I wanted to be the kind of hardworking, productive employee I'd been before. The one who hardly ever missed a detail and was always ten steps ahead of whatever came next. I wanted to be the kind of writer who could dedicate hours every day to making her dream come true.

The reality is, most days, I was none of this. Or at least, I didn't feel like it.

It wasn't that I wasn't receiving praise both at home and at work, because I was. But I realized that just wasn't enough. Because to me, it felt like most days I was trying to show up everywhere, and as a result of my trying so hard, I showed up nowhere. I spent a lot of time crying to myself, often when no one was looking. I was confused and frustrated with myself because there was a lot of goodness in my life, yet I still felt sad. I felt completely overwhelmed. I did my best to hold it together and put on a brave face. But occasionally tears broke free when someone asked the wrong question at the wrong time. I can tell you that my poor boss sometimes never saw what was coming, and my poor husband must have felt like he was walking on eggshells half the time.

I truly felt like there had to be something wrong with me. After all, so many women and men had figured out how to juggle all of life's responsibilities and blessings without the help and support I had. And most of them made it look easy.

When Michael would come home after work, I'd put on a brave face and smile like everything was okay. I was desperate to give him the happiest home and life he'd ever experienced, and I never wanted my personal feelings to compromise that. When people asked me how I was doing, I would smile confidently and tell them I was great. Because again, *there was* a lot of greatness in my life, which made it that much more difficult to explain the sadness.

One day, after months of feeling this way and shortly after the conversation with my brother, I reached a breaking point. I was tired of feeling sad. I was tired of keeping my walls up and pretending that everything was okay. I was not okay. When I finally decided to open up to Michael about how I was feeling, the flood of relief that followed was amazing. I called it "letting the bad air out." It didn't immediately solve my problems, but it felt good to be both supported and reminded about what I was capable of, and of how much I was loved.

I started answering the question honestly when people asked how I was doing. I told them the truth about my struggles and how I was feeling and, in return, they often expressed similar feelings and words of support. In fact, one of my best friends, Sarah, was going through something extremely similar at the time. Suddenly, it didn't feel like *just* me. I didn't feel so lonely.

I also reached out for professional help. I started seeing a therapist and, little by little, I started to readjust the standards I'd once held or envisioned for myself. Most importantly, *I gave it to God*. I realized that part of my struggles originated from my desire to control and predict every outcome. *Are you sensing a theme here?* As best as I could, I gave that to Him. I also realized that a big part of my problem was that I was afraid of failing. So, I gave that fear to him too.

I did my very best to give it all to God—the good, the bad, the uncertain, and everything in between. When I did this, it didn't change my circumstances, but I did feel noticeably better. Noticeably happier and definitely more at peace.

What I realized is that there really was not any other choice. Because as much as I would like to have the balancing act figured out by now, I don't. And as much as I would like to be able to predict how everything will turn out, I can't. But here is what I do know.

Like Ryan, my tendency is to shield the people I love from my less-than-perfect parts. From the parts that feel dark and lonely. When things feel ridiculously hard, or when I feel irrationally sad, my natural reaction is to put a smile on my face, make a joke, and keep on moving. After all, the last thing I ever want to do is bring people down with me. *But letting people in is a lot different from letting people down.*

It was so easy that day for me to tell Ryan that he should let people support him, but it was exponentially more difficult to accept that advice for myself. Similarly, I thought it was crazy that my brother could not recognize how amazing and loved he truly was. Yet here I was struggling with the same exact thing. So many people were telling me I was doing a great job at all of the things, but it felt like I couldn't receive their praise and was constantly falling short of my vision for myself. I still don't know why.

But I do know that life feels better when it's shared with others. When we learn to give it to God.

I realized that telling someone to let their walls down is a lot easier than allowing my own walls to fall, and that, sometimes, life brings us moments that are disguised as helping others so that we can be reminded of the help that we need ourselves.

Thank you, Ryan.

Dear Little Bee,

I hope you emulate your uncle in so many ways.

I want you to be a protector.

I want you to be loyal to those you love.

I want you to be the recipient of the phone call someone makes when they need a friend.

I want you to be unapologetically yourself, no matter what.

Little Bee, I want you to know that it is okay not to always feel okay. When you are feeling down, or less than, just remember that there are a lot of people in this world who are standing by waiting to love and support you. And a lot of people who, with the invitation, will remind you of how amazing and loved you truly are. So let your walls down.

And lastly, Little Bee, life can be pretty overwhelming. Even when things are going well, it might still feel like a lot to handle. When this happens, I want you to remember who is ultimately in control, and give it all to Him. He's got you, Little Bee.

Verses for When You're Feeling Overwhelmed

Therefore, do not worry about tomorrow, for tomorrow will worry about itself. Each day has enough trouble of its own. (Matthew 6:34 NIV)

Cast your worries upon him because he cares for you. (1 Peter 5:7 NABRE)

Questions for When You're Feeling Overwhelmed

- What about your situation can you control?
- Do you have a trusted friend or loved one you could talk to about whatever it is you're facing?
- What can you pray about instead of worrying about?

When the dance feels overwhelming,
God is only just beginning.

17

WHEN YOU WANT TO CONNECT YOUR LIFE'S DOTS

Learn to Dance

This last person I will write about is someone I grew up believing I knew. At a relatively young age, this individual was so sure of herself. She had a plan for her life. A plan that involved getting a great-paying job and marrying the man of her dreams. Once. The plan demanded both perfection and knowing, and it never made room for second-guessing. It was a blueprint centered around what she thought she knew, and its execution was motivated by fear and hard work. Her plan was built from both the opinions of her life and her vision for it.

And then those plans changed. In some ways, and by some standards, those plans even failed. It was a season of her life that she swore against and never saw coming, but now, it's a season she can't imagine her life without.

She said goodbye to the person she loved most and, although it was an expected part of her life, it was unexpectedly painful. She made honest and hard decisions that made her feel lost and ashamed. And then she fell in love with someone who didn't initially make a lot of sense, someone who wasn't part of the original plan but who changed her heart and mind against all odds. That was a decision both freeing and terrifying all at once. Most importantly, she learned to love God and, through His grace and mercy, began a life for herself she'd never envisioned but realized she had always wanted.

She did not always know she wanted to be a mom. Part of her doubted her practical ability to take care of another human; the other part wondered if she could ever love someone more than she loved herself. It was both a selfish and an honest reality that she pondered.

For nine months, she carried a baby inside of her. She prayed every single day and night for God to protect him and allow her to become the mom she didn't know she wanted to be. All the while, she was afraid to let her heart love him for fear that maybe he wouldn't come true.

We spent over thirty years together, so I thought I knew exactly who she was. But truthfully, I had no idea. Because on November 8, 2022, I finally met her. The *new her* for the first time.

November 8, 2022, was the day I became a mom. Within moments of my son Braxton's arrival, I knew I'd already come so far. That every single step and misstep had led me to this moment. It was clear that my journey was already worth it, yet somehow was just beginning. I quickly fell in love with the belief that hard seasons are the best teachers, and that the lessons I learned from many seasons were a gift that I could give.

In our first few months of becoming acquainted with each other, my son challenged everything I'd once believed to be true. I was amazed at how naturally being a mom came to me. Loving and caring for my baby felt as easy as breathing. I became even more dependent on my relationship with God and even prouder of the life I was building with my husband.

I dug deep and prayed hard for purpose. In some ways, I was still working on healing, while in other ways I could feel the smoldering heat around me as I rose from the ashes to begin again.

It was then, when I closed my eyes at night and prayed to God for direction and purpose, that I felt Him tell me I already had it. I looked back on my relatively short life and found both my confidence and my calling. I forgave myself for everything I didn't know or hadn't done right, and I learned to appreciate the people and experiences in my life and the goodness they shared. Even if it wasn't always easy.

As I did this, I both embraced my own story and started to write it again. And then I kept writing. I realized that despite my doubts, insecurities, and self-proclaimed shortcomings, God had been equipping me all along. He had placed beautiful people and meaningful experiences in my life, and both had given me an extraordinary amount of knowledge. Knowledge that I think is worth sharing.

Because this knowledge *was* needed; it *is* needed. It made me a better mom, wife, daughter, and friend. And if I had to do it all again to learn these lessons, I would.

Like a bee who dances to help other bees survive, this is my dance for you.

Dear Little Bee,

I know, learning from your parents might not always feel like something you can or want to do, but trust me, it isn't as terrible as it might seem. I am just praying that I teach you and prepare you well.

It is the most important job I will ever have. That is what moms are for.

Our hard seasons are often our best teachers, but all seasons have something to offer. And the lessons we learn are meant to be shared with others. Be a funnel for good and remember these things:

Embrace and trust your hive.

You are blessed with an amazing family, one that will always be standing in your corner but may not always be here on this earth to cheer you on. Some you have read about here, others you have not. But you won't have to read about them to understand just how amazing they all are. Families can be tough, but I would not trade ours for the world. Please take the time to get to know them and love them for all they are.

Who you choose to invite into your hive is equally as important as who is already there. If you are lucky, you will spend a lifetime meeting different, amazing, and downright difficult people. Let them all in. Don't stop at what feels familiar; dream bigger.

Stay on high alert, Little Bee. Let people know you, challenge you, and support you. Whenever you are feeling inferior, remember that you have something to learn. Listen to their stories, and share yours when the time is right. And please, take every moment for what it is worth. Stop to smell the roses. Don't waste a moment that this life gives you; there is beauty in all.

Sometimes life just stings.

Above all, I need you to know how much you are loved by God, no matter what. He has a plan for your life. Remember, He isn't asking you to figure it out; He's asking you to trust that He already has.

When you make mistakes or question yourself, remember that the most powerful choice you can make is to learn what you can, move forward, and try your hardest to do better the next time. The devil will be fighting relentlessly to keep you in your past, but God is much more interested in your future. Reach for His hand, and move forward.

Sometimes you will have to make tough decisions. Oftentimes people will formulate their opinions about those decisions. You don't need anyone's validation, Little Bee. Look in the mirror—you've got this, and I've always got you.

Tough times are inevitable, but you are strong. You are a sword, but you are also human.

Little Bee, I can't promise you that your path will be easy. In fact, I can almost guarantee that there will be times where it won't be. But that's okay. The path forward isn't always the easiest one. And the easiest path isn't often the most fulfilling journey.

I wouldn't trade the love your dad and I share for anything. Little Bee, I love him more than any of my words could ever explain, but I do hope that you grow up witnessing first-hand what real love looks like. Your dad has shown me the value of communication, trust, and faith in a relationship, and that real love is worth waiting for. Your dad helped me find my faith and also the most authentic version of myself I have ever known.

If you ever find yourself in a position where you feel like you have to start over again, just remember that our God is a God of second chances. His mercy and grace are new every single morning. Seek out the people who remind you of that.

Take flight when the timing is right.

As you take flight, trust that you are far more capable than you likely give yourself credit for. Have confidence, but stay *humble. You will never be too old or too wise to learn something new. Everything you are experiencing, you are ultimately learning, and what you are learning is powerful.*

Similarly, your time, words, and energy are some of the most powerful resources you will ever possess, and they can never be taken back, so choose them wisely. Where you choose to invest your energy ultimately decides how you will live your life. I pray that you will live your life on purpose and that you will invest these invaluable resources wisely, Little Bee.

Don't forget to assume goodness and competence of others. The world doesn't need any more critics or people who think they know better. The world needs your kindness and your grace. You need your own kindness and grace.

And when all else fails, give it to God, Little Bee. He knows the desires of your heart better than you do. I promise.

Verses for When You Want to Connect Your Life's Dots

Keep your minds on whatever is true, pure, right, holy, friendly, and proper. (Philippians 4:8 CEV)

Many are the plans of the human heart, but it is the decision of the LORD that endures. (Proverbs 19:21 NABRE)

And we know that all things work together for good for those who love God. (Romans 8:28 NET)

Questions for When You Want to Connect Your Life's Dots

- What is something significant that you've been through?
- What did that experience teach you?
- What would you tell someone else who is going through something similar?

The world is your stage—dance away.

EPILOGUE

THE DANCE THAT NEVER REALLY ENDS

I Still Don't Have It All Figured Out

I think that most people decide to write a book because they believe they have arrived at a conclusion worth sharing. Or maybe because they have survived incredible hardship or achieved celebrity status. Therefore, I'm assuming that most readers pick up a book when they believe the pages contain the answers to the questions they have or the best-kept secrets to success. Or maybe when they just want to be swept away by history or entertainment.

You may have figured this out by now, but I am not that author, and I sincerely hope you are not that reader. Because if you are, chances are you stopped reading long before arriving at this page. And that, I am told, is not good for book reviews.

Assuming that we are still walking this journey together, I want to leave you where we began. I started writing a very different version of this book when I was going through a divorce. I was twenty-eight years old, and at the time I felt in my heart that the things I was going through and dealing with could not be unique to me. I was encouraged by people who agreed and who thought that other people in similar situations might find encouragement or relatability in my story.

And then I put the pen down—hard. Because my divorce was not something I felt should be celebrated or glamorized. I also began to recognize it as just a single chapter of my entire story. Furthermore, I am not an expert on marriage or divorce, and the last thing I wanted someone to do was to take my advice. The hard and honest truth is, I still have no idea if what I did and how I handled things were right or wrong.

I just know that they were the best I could do at the given time. I know that I learned something from that experience. And I know that ultimately, God worked it all out for good. For that, I am grateful.

As the years passed, the voice in my heart nagging me to write never quieted. I loved storytelling and I had a passion for it. I distracted myself for long enough by helping other people tell their stories, and every time I did, I felt a joy in my heart that indicated I was working in the right direction.

With time and prayer, I realized it was time to pick up the pen again. But this time, what I was writing would be much less about me or a specific event, and more about the goodness that had been brought to my life and how I could use my talents to help pay that forward. To be a funnel for good.

At that point, I knew that the most important person who would ever read anything I chose to write would be my son. But that realization and this opportunity would have never existed without the hard times. Divorce, death, and insecurities included. Because hard seasons have a way of making or breaking you. And even if they break you, they have a weird way of rebuilding you— typically stronger than ever before. They stop you in your tracks and take you to your knees. They make you question everything, including yourself.

Hard seasons are also our best teachers, but all seasons have something to offer.

I realize that a lot of people have survived far more difficult things than what I've been through. But that is also why this book is not about the things I've been through. It's about the people and the lessons who were always there along the way.

This is a story about a woman who allowed her own hard seasons to be her greatest teacher. It is a love letter from a mom, who wants to share what she has learned, no matter how small or obvious it may be, to create an even better life for her son. But the learning and sharing did not stop when the writing began. In fact, as the writing began, the learning was just getting started. As I got more serious about writing, it was amazing how much I was discovering. It was not uncommon for me to be working on a chapter and subsequently find myself needing to be reminded of the exact lesson I was sharing.

Which brings me to my second point. You may already know everything you need to know in order to do better. You might just need to take yourself on an introspective journey to be reminded of it. More than that, what you know and what you have learned can help others. In fact, it should. I hope you've figured this out. It is the whole premise of *The Waggle Dance.*

I have no doubt that my learnings are only just beginning, and truthfully, I am still just doing my best to figure it all out. I don't have all the answers, the rule book, or the ability to predict what might happen next. None of us do. *But that is what life is for.*

Life is for the figuring it out—the loving, the messing up, and the waking up every day grateful that you get the chance to try it all again. So here's to hoping. Here's to always learning. Here's to kindness and to sharing. Here's to the chapters that have been written and the ones we don't yet know.

And most of all, Little Bee, here's to you. Thanks for making me a mom.

Dear Little Bee,

If there ever comes a time when I am not here to tell you myself, I want you to know that you have brought more love and purpose to my life than I could have ever imagined. You have made it all make sense. Now, I want you to start dancing— and don't ever stop.

Will you dance with me?
Love,
Mom